Housewives & Repairmen
"the Untold Secrets"
True Stories as they actually happened!
Husbands leave for work and their wives stay home to be "Serviced"!!

Michael C. Riley

Service Technician

HousewivesandRepairmen.com

www.CreateSpace.com

Housewives & Repairmen
"the Untold Secrets"
True Stories as they actually happened!
Husbands leave for work and their wives stay home to be "Serviced"!!

Library of Congress
Copyright Office
101 Independence Avenue S.E.
Washington D.C. 20559-6000
Register of Copyrights, United States of America
TX 6-062-162

Covers Designed by Michael C. Riley
Additional Proofing of book by Kimberly K. Riley

CreateSpace.com - "Self-Published" Book
Manufactured in the United States of America

Library of Congress Cataloging in Publication Data

Riley, Michael C. (Michael Claude)

ISBN
0-9765524-0-X

Housewives & Repairmen
"the Untold Secrets"
True Stories as they actually happened!
Husbands leave for work and their wives stay home to be "Serviced"!!

I dedicate this book to the inspiration given to me by my son, Jason, and my whole family who have always been there for me, through the tough times, as well as the fun times.

I especially tribute my book to my twin, Patrick, although his life was short lived, he always showed me by example, that exemplifying Great Integrity is First and Foremost. The way my twin Patrick touched me with his gentle, but solid integrity, made his short time on earth one of my most precious and endearing gifts I could ever expect, and I will always cherish his memory with not only the greatest of admiration, but with the utmost respect, until the end of my time.

Of course, most importantly, I must tribute this book wholeheartedly to the woman, our Mother, who not only gave birth to us twins, Pat & I (the 3rd one, our triplet, was stillborn), but also to three other older siblings. My Mother's undying dedication to her five children with no father present, showed great challenges at times for all of us, but she never showed any abandoning of strength in her commitment towards all of us, and strongly instilled the severe importance of manners, respect, and Integrity. Through her selflessness, I was able to take what she taught me and make it through the maze of my twenty years of women's inappropriateness, while doing service calls, somewhat unscathed. For my Mother's great integrity, I thank her dearly, for teaching me not only right from wrong, but also that you must believe in who you are and never allow someone else to lead you astray from your path of common decency.

Housewives & Repairmen
"the Untold Secrets"
True Stories as they actually happened!
Husbands leave for work and their wives stay home to be "Serviced"!!

Housewives & Repairmen
"the Untold Secrets"
True Stories as they actually happened!
Husbands leave for work and their wives stay home to be "Serviced"!!

In the Very Beginning
Excitement about a New Career:
I was a young adult male, 20 years of age
and newly married when I lost my job at a
furniture warehouse. I had worked part time
while going to Arizona State University where
I was enrolled in the Electrical Engineering
College. After meeting and deciding to marry
a front office girl at the furniture store, we
arrived back home to Mesa, Arizona from our
honeymoon in Fern Grotto, Kauai. It was
then I was notified I no longer had a job. The
company had an unwritten rule that stated,
no one could be married to another employee
and still remain working for them. Losing my job,
being newly married, and going to school, would
prove to be a very rough start to our marriage.
I was lucky enough to have talked to one of
my sisters that had a friend who worked at an
appliance repair facility in Phoenix. I was
offered an apprenticeship to perform in-shop
appliance repairs in order to learn the
appliance repair trade. I accepted
immediately, knowing that I had always been
mechanically inclined and loved to fix things.
I started right away, I fit right in and felt at
home diagnosing and repairing appliances,
microwaves and refrigeration products.

Housewives & Repairmen
"the Untold Secrets"
True Stories as they actually happened!
Husbands leave for work and their wives stay home to be "Serviced"!!

After about 3 months, of a 6 month probation period, I was asked if I thought I was ready to get out of the shop and go on the road to do in-home service calls. I jumped at the opportunity and never turned back. Due to lack of proper management when I started, I filed a complaint against the company in a verbal session and was asked to leave the company, in no uncertain terms.

An associate contacted me, having recognized my abilities in the service and repair industry, about a position with a large appliance Corporation. The representative gave his condolences for my removal from the prior company, but had a better offer for me to work as a service tech for a major corporation of appliances in Detroit. I accepted immediately and my new wife and I were on our way to Detroit to start a new life. I had been in this service technician job for about 18 months, when I was approached about a promotion for a management position in Benton Harbor, Michigan. Right about the same time we had our son who was a joyous addition to our lives. I accepted the challenge and passed the test of the interviews. We were now on our way to Benton Harbor, Michigan to start my new management job

Housewives & Repairmen
"the Untold Secrets"
True Stories as they actually happened!
Husbands leave for work and their wives stay home to be "Serviced"!!

with the appliance Corporation. After about 8 months, I gave up my position in management due to my wife's yearning to be back home in Arizona. We moved back where we proceeded to get a divorce.

Soon after my divorce, I started my own appliance service repair business contracting with a company out of Arizona. After a few years, another corporation approached me to be their National Trainer, to travel and train their technicians. I accepted the position and trained technicians throughout the United States for about 2 years. I got tired of all the travel, so I took a position in San Diego with one of their service centers as an independent service contractor and was there for about 4 1/2 years.

Shortly after meeting someone that I cared a great deal about, we moved to NW Chicago. I started a new business in Graphic Design and Programming to finally make use of my schooling at ASU. I am currently a graphic designer and programmer, but will always be a technician at heart.

Housewives & Repairmen
"the Untold Secrets"
True Stories as they actually happened!
Husbands leave for work and their wives stay home to be "Serviced"!!

Long and Frustrating Challenges:

In the appliance service field it can be extreme
frustrating when you first start out. You don't
have the knowledge of all the product lines as
well as the seasoned veteran service
technicians. I went through many challenges a
times of total frustration not really knowing wha
was doing and having to constantly ask the
advice of someone that had been doing service
for a longer period than myself.

One of the difficult things about being a new gu
in the service field is that not every service mar
will share information with you. There is a
mentality in some service technicians, an
attitude of their personal pride of learning it
themselves and they want you to learn it yours
as well. This can be extremely frustrating,
because the customer is the one that suffers
when you are not correct in your diagnosis and
repair procedure. One thing is for sure, once yc
make the mistake, you don't ever make it again
You also get that personal satisfaction by
learning it yourself. You have solved the proble
on your own and it means so much more, but it
can definitely be said that it can be humiliating
and very frustrating following this path. I later
found when I was a National Trainer, that I real
enjoyed sharing with technicians the knowledge

Housewives & Repairmen
"the Untold Secrets"
True Stories as they actually happened!
Husbands leave for work and their wives stay home to be "Serviced"!!

could pass on to them to make life much easier regarding the servicing of customers appliances. I guess the best of both worlds is a great mixture for every technician to learn by. That way, you learn it can always be difficult at times to diagnose, and you must rely on your talents, knowledge and experience with good common sense always at hand. Every good technician has great mechanical abilities and good common sense or they don't last.

Housewives & Repairmen
"the Untold Secrets"
True Stories as they actually happened!
Husbands leave for work and their wives stay home to be "Serviced"!!

The Pay-Off:

The great customers I met and being able to solve the problems with their appliances, was the biggest pay-off I received in all of my years of doing repair service. There is no better feelin than to walk into a customer's home, that is ver cold from no heat, or laundry is piled up from th lack of a working clothes washer, and you are able to put a smile back on the customer's face by the time you leave. This gives you the ultimate feeling of accomplishment and person satisfaction, knowing that the distraught customer now has their lifestyle back to the way it was before they needed your services. The feeling of satisfaction and self worth is tremendous, when you walk out of a customer's house, seeing them smile and sometimes very ecstatic about being able to continue washing that huge pile of dirty clothes.

10

Housewives & Repairmen
"the Untold Secrets"
True Stories as they actually happened!
Husbands leave for work and their wives stay home to be "Serviced"!!

Backyard Lady

I was to arrive at a service call on an oven that did not heat anymore. This appeared to be a very trivial service call after looking at the work order, but I was about to encounter something I truly was not ready to deal with. I had only been on the road as a technician for approximately, two weeks. It was a very hot day, about 115 degrees, in the middle of the summer, which was not unusual for a summer day in Arizona. In fact, as I was to find out in years to come, most technicians look forward to the heat and the flesh.

I arrived at the home of a middle-aged woman that was quite attractive, along with her slightly large frame and friendly nature. I was welcomed into her home and escorted to her kitchen, where the oven I was to work on was located. This nice lady finally introduced herself as Karen, and began to explain the problem she was having with her oven. I listened very intently, as not to miss any little details that would make diagnosing the oven easier. As soon as Karen had shared her displeasure with the oven not working, she exited the room to allow me to find the problem. I proceeded to diagnose the oven, and found that the oven igniter had failed. I reassembled the oven and called for Karen, to

Housewives & Repairmen
the Untold Secrets
True Stories as they actually happened!
Husbands leave for work and their wives stay home to be "Serviced"!!

give her the bad news that I would have to order
the part and come back to fix her oven.
She was very nice about my not having the part
and commented that she doesn't cook much in
the summer, because it gets her too hot! S he
had quite a smile on her face, and I was curious
about the way that she made her statement.
It was now two days later, and I was going back
to install the oven igniter in Karen's oven. I called
Karen on the way over to her home, and told her
I would be there in approximately 15 minutes.
She told me that she would be there, and hung
up.
As I pulled into her driveway, I noticed that
the garage door was open. On the door, inside
the garage, was a piece of paper that looked like
a note. My first impression was that she had to
leave and left me a note informing me of this. I
started to get irritated that I drove all the way to
her home and she had left. I parked my van and
walked into the garage to read the note on the
entry door into her home. The note read as
follows: Warning--I'm in the back yard
sunbathing, please come in! I wasn't sure at this
point why Karen had written Warning on the
note. I must have stood at the door about two
minutes before I knocked. I received no answer
and I proceeded to open the door slowly, feeling

Housewives & Repairmen
"the Untold Secrets"
True Stories as they actually happened!
Husbands leave for work and their wives stay home to be "Serviced"!!

like I was walking into someone's house
uninvited.

When I had opened the door all the way, I
noticed through the kitchen and living room, I
could see out the sliding glass doors into the
backyard. To my complete surprise, Karen was
sprawled out on a lounge chair, completely
nude. I began thinking to myself that I didn't
know how I was going to get her attention
without her knowing that I had seen her. Well, I
wasn't going to have to worry about it, because
she sat up all of a sudden, smiled and waved.
Karen came inside and greeted me after she put
on her very tight-fitting shorts and halter-top. As
she walked towards me, saying how nice it was
outdoors to get a tan, I noticed her nipples were
very erect through the thin material of the halter
top.

It was very difficult at this time to concentrate on
the reason I had come to her home in the first
place. I nervously started conversation with her,
and began repairing the oven. Karen seated
herself about five feet away from me at the
kitchen table. She was still talking about anything
and everything, which just went in one ear and
out the other. I was so nervous, I could hardly
concentrate when she explained that she was a
nudist, and so was her son. She then pointed her

Housewives & Repairmen
"the Untold Secrets"
True Stories as they actually happened!
Husbands leave for work and their wives stay home to be "Serviced"!!

son out in the backyard, where he was still weed-whacking the lawn. Karen stated that she hoped this did not make me uncomfortable. I responded that it didn't, but I don't think I was very convincing with such a shaky voice.

I finished the repair on Karen's oven, and all th small talk that made me so nervous, and prepared to leave. Karen walked me to the doc after paying the bill. She was a very nice lady with a lifestyle that I had never been introduced to, until that moment. As I left, I can remember how thrilling and nerve racking this experience was at the same time. As soon as I got into my van, I called my buddy and told him about this wild experience, but never told him how nervou I felt!

Housewives & Repairmen
"the Untold Secrets"
True Stories as they actually happened!
Husbands leave for work and their wives stay home to be "Serviced"!!

Young' in

It was late summer in the north suburbs of
Detroit, when I was about to run into one of the
most dangerous situations a service technician
can be un-fairly faced with. A young girl, under
the age of 18 had called for un-needed service
on her dishwasher. I was about to be put in the
most uncomfortable and shocking situation of my
entire life.

I headed out from the service branch to go work,
on yet another seemingly straightforward and
easy service call on a dishwasher. As I drove to
the customer's house, I was reading the
complaint on the service order. The complaint
was that the dishwasher did not get anything
wet, which sounded real simple when I thought
about it. There was probably no water coming
into the dishwasher, which would be a quick call.
The house was about an hour out of the city, and
it seemed like forever to get there. When I
arrived, there were no cars in the driveway, so I
figured right away, I must have made the long
trip for nothing.

I walked up to the door and rang the doorbell,
after about two minutes a young girl came to the
door and parted the drape inside to look out. She
said, "Are you here to fix the dishwasher"? I
replied, "Yes, Miss, I am". She promptly opened

Housewives & Repairmen
"the Untold Secrets"
True Stories as they actually happened!
Husbands leave for work and their wives stay home to be "Serviced"!!

the door and to my astonishment had on a white
see-thru French bikini. I immediately felt my
heart pounding out of my chest, and the anxiety
just hit me. I muttered, "Is your Mother or Father
home"? She responded quickly, saying, "My
mother said she would be back in five minutes
and to let you in to fix the dishwasher"! I thought
about it for a moment and against my better
judgment went inside.

This young girl had to be 13 years of age,
dressed inappropriately like an 18 year-old! I was
so nervous being in the house alone with her,
and anticipated her Mother's arrival asap. She
pointed to the direction of the dishwasher and I
followed her to the kitchen. Her body was
covered with oil, as she apparently had been
lying out sunbathing. As we walked through the
hall to the kitchen, I finally spotted the
dishwasher, and thought to myself, I need to fix
this and get the hell out of here! I asked her what
the problem with the dishwasher was, and she
smiled and said, "It doesn't get wet by itself"!
Only adding to my displeasure by her actions for
such a young child, if only her Mother knew,
which I hoped would arrive soon and address
her about her very inappropriate actions!

16

Housewives & Repairmen
"the Untold Secrets"
True Stories as they actually happened!
Husbands leave for work and their wives stay home to be "Serviced"!!

I immediately went to the valve under the sink,
extremely uncomfortable now, to make sure the
water was turned on to the dishwasher. Darn it, it
was on!

So now, I was faced with lying down on the floor
to access the lower front panel and check the
water valve, after I checked the float. I checked
the float and it was working. I was not looking
forward to lying on the floor in front of the
dishwasher, because the kitchen was so small.
She was sitting backwards on one of the kitchen
table chairs, with her legs wrapped around the
outsides of the back of the chair, facing me. I
took off the lower front panel of the dishwasher
and asked her "Where is your mother, I thought
you said five minutes". She quickly replied, "She
will be here any minute". I was thinking, GOD, I
hope so!

All of a sudden, she stood up and walked
towards me as I was lying on my back, trying to
check the water valve under the dishwasher. I
thought I was going to throw-up, as she stepped
over the top of my body to reach into the
cabinets above, to get a glass. I thought my
heart was going to pound out of my chest!

I was now only thinking of how quick I could get
out of the house, as these absolutely
inappropriate actions of this child had just

17

Housewives & Repairmen
"the Untold Secrets"
True Stories as they actually happened!
Husbands leave for work and their wives stay home to be "Serviced"!!

sickened me, more than I had ever been before
She bent down and asked, "Would you like
something to drink", with a bigger smile on her
face this time? I answered quickly, "No thanks"!
As she went back and sat down in the chair as
she was before, I got out from under the
dishwasher and turned it on. I had not turned it
on before, as I was so nervous, and now had
found nothing wrong with any of its parts. There
was water coming in immediately! I put the
panel back on, and told her, "It works now and
will get the dishes nice and wet and clean---No
charge", saying this as I was practically
running out the front door.
I was so worked up with disgust when I got to m
van, I actually felt sick to my stomach. This little
girl just had fun at my expense and time, and I
actually was quite upset! I had spent an hour
driving, and she had put me in an awkward
position as a professional. All I can say is that
she is lucky it was a gentleman like me, and not
some pervert or rapist that had come to her doo
I would never go into another customers house
from that point forward, unless an adult 18
years or older was home!
This kind of thing does happen, and we service
technicians don't need the trouble it can bring! I
will go so far as to say, that this kind of behavio

Housewives & Repairmen
"the Untold Secrets"
True Stories as they actually happened!
Husbands leave for work and their wives stay home to be "Serviced"!!

today can lead to real trouble for young girls, and service technicians! Please, don't do it! Please Mothers and Fathers, know what your children are doing and keep them safe from all those sick individuals out there who would harm your child!

Housewives & Repairmen
"the Untold Secrets"
True Stories as they actually happened!
Husbands leave for work and their wives stay home to be "Serviced"!!

Three BJ's

It was a regular service day, and I was headed to a service call on a washing machine that wa not draining the water out. I soon arrived at the customer's house, which was not the best maintained yard or well kept driveway on the block. There was an old Chevy in the driveway and the house was in poor shape, requiring pa and a new roof. The house was located in Tempe, Arizona, not too far from the University I pulled up to the house and had the feeling rig away, that I may not be able to sell this repair due to the shambles of the unkempt house. I thought to myself, that I shouldn't judge the situation too, because I knew that everyone deserved professional repair service, regardles of how much money they may have. I knew tha had adjusted the price in the past, so a custom could afford the repair, which always made me feel like I was being very fair to those less fortunate. I didn't mind losing a little of my profi to satisfy a customer.

I walked up the driveway, through the mess of newspaper and car parts, to the side entrance the house. After knocking o n the door, I was greeted by a very pleasant larger framed young lady. At the same time the door opened, I immediately heard crying from a baby in the

20

Housewives & Repairmen
"the Untold Secrets"
True Stories as they actually happened!
Husbands leave for work and their wives stay home to be "Serviced"!!

background and saw kids running around in the
kitchen in their underwear. The nice young lady
invited me in, and proceeded in the direction of
where the washing machine was located. All the
way to the machine she was explaining what the
problem with the washer was, as I listened
intently. Upon arriving at the washer on the
backyard porch, I assured her I would locate the
problem quickly and give her an estimate.

As I was diagnosing the washer, the young lady
continued to talk about anything and everything.
She was repeatedly telling me that she had six
kids and her husband had left her. She told me
repeatedly that she was on welfare and didn't
have very much money, but that she had to have
the washer fixed, because all of the kid's clothes
were dirty. I kept assuring her that the problem
was not very bad, that it was probably only the
water pump, and that it would be much cheaper
than buying a new washer. I verified that the
pump was indeed bad and worked up a price
that was considerably lower than my normal
price for the repair. Thinking that my quote was
extremely fair, not leaving hardly any margin for
profit for myself, I gave her the estimated cost to
replace the pump.

I was confident she could afford the price of the
repair I had quoted her, when she responds that,

Housewives & Repairmen
"the Untold Secrets"
True Stories as they actually happened!
Husbands leave for work and their wives stay home to be "Serviced"!!

there was no way she had that much money! This nice young lady was faced with a dilemma her kids had no clothes to wear, because they were all dirty. I stood before her with an air of silence, and I didn't know what to say. There was no way I could do the repair for any cheaper, or I would lose money. She then told me to hold on for a minute, that she would be right back. I told her I would be right there by the washing machine until she came back. I was now actually feeling a little better about my estimate to fix her washer, get paid and be on my way. She came back in just about a minute, with a very serious look on her face, and told me that she would give me three blowjobs, in exchange for the replacing the pump on the washing machine.

I was shocked and dumb-founded by her forwardness and bluntness, not knowing what to say at first. I finally regained my composure and initial shock, and told her that I could not do that. I told her I would need to collect money for the repair or I would get into trouble, trying to change the focus away from her proposition. I was feeling bad for her desperation, but at the same time I was getting upset that she had wasted my time, and didn't appear to have any money at all, anyways.

Housewives & Repairmen
"the Untold Secrets"
True Stories as they actually happened!
Husbands leave for work and their wives stay home to be "Serviced"!!

She then stated to me that she would have a friend replace the pump on the washer, and that she would pay me for the service call. As I was leaving, I told her to have a nice day, having mixed emotions about her proposition and the predicament she was in with her six kids. All things considered, I assured myself that I had done the right thing!

As I walked out to my service truck, I felt very sad that a woman would have to go to such an extreme low, to provide the necessity of having clean clothes for her children. This customer forever changed my compassion for those less fortunate that struggle to maintain a standard household for their children, at all costs.

Housewives & Repairmen
"the Untold Secrets"
True Stories as they actually happened!
Husbands leave for work and their wives stay home to be "Serviced"!!

Three's a Show

It is a typical foggy morning in San Diego. I am getting ready for another day of pleasant weather once the fog burns off, somewhere between 10:00a.m. and 12:00 noon. I am collecting my parts for the day and routing my calls in a logical order to run them. It is going to be another beautiful day running calls down by the ocean. I get to my very first call of the day, which happens to be a washing machine that is not completing the cycle. I have a very difficult time finding a place to park down by the ocean every time I do calls in this area. I finally find a place to park and have to walk about a half mile to get to my first customers house. This has caused me to be running about thirty minutes late from what my arrival time should have been and I am thinking that right away the customer is going to be upset with me.

I finally reach the front door of their beachfront condo, over-looking the ocean on the 22nd floor of this huge high-rise complex of condos. I ring the doorbell several times, which sounds like church bells chiming, and after about two minutes the customer finally answers the door. A very attractive middle -aged lady greets me, and I state I am there to service her washing machine.

Housewives & Repairmen
"the Untold Secrets"

True Stories as they actually happened!

Husbands leave for work and their wives stay home to be "Serviced"!!

She says that she will show me where it is and invites me in. I follow her down a long hall and around through a maze until we finally arrive at the laundry room. There, her husband is standing and we greet each other good morning. I turn my attention back to the Mrs. who is standing next to the washing machine telling me that it does not work right.

At this time, I step up to the front of the washer and start to ask her questions about what exactly the machine is doing or not doing. She states that the washer did not rinse out her clothes. With this, I have been prompted to ask her many questions to pinpoint what exactly she means by does not rinse out the clothes. In my mind, I know that can mean about ten different things, depending on her exact explanation of the problem. I really start to grill her gently, about whether she means there is still soap in the clothes, soaking wet clothes at the end of the cycle or water still left in the tub when it is done. She states she is not sure, at the end of the cycle they are not rinsed out, which is very vague to a service technician.

At this point, I mention to her that I will check the operation and determine what the problem is and I will inform her when I find the problem. The Mrs. steps back a step and the husband is still

Housewives & Repairmen
"the Untold Secrets"
True Stories as they actually happened!
Husbands leave for work and their wives stay home to be "Serviced"!!

lurking behind me about 10 steps straight back
start to cycle the washer and the Mrs. reaches
over my right shoulder with her right hand,
brushing my right shoulder with her left breast,
which is very healthy indeed. Thinking this is a
accident; I just reposition myself slightly left to
take the pressure of her breast off my right
shoulder. She is trying to tell me that I need to
turn the timer knob to a certain spot while
reaching over my shoulder, to turn the knob
herself. After listening to her and allowing her t
turn the knob herself while I step out of her way
she tells me that this position she has set it at,
where the problem is.

I step back toward the washer and start it, agai
checking the operation in this cycle. Once agai
she reaches over my shoulder and really pushe
her left breast very firmly up against my
shoulder. Now I am getting nervous, because
now in my mind, this is not an accident.
Remembering that her husband is standing
behind us about ten steps, I move away to the
left again and glance back. The husband is
standing behind me watching what his wife is
doing, and has a smile on his face. He does nc
say a word, just smiles. I don't know what to
think at this point, and part of me just wants to
get the hell out of there. I control myself, and

Housewives & Repairmen
"the Untold Secrets"
True Stories as they actually happened!
Husbands leave for work and their wives stay home to be "Serviced"!!

resume my place in front of the washer after she has repositioned the timer knob to a different cycle.

Once again, I started the washer to look for a problem in the operation and the Mrs. reaches over again and starts to rub her breast back and forth on my shoulder. This time I definitely knew it was not an accident and moved away real quick letting her know that I do not like this, especially in front of her husband, who is now grinning. I now tell her that if she let's me just run the different cycles without changing the knob position at all, I will find the problem quicker, and I will let her know when I find it. She gets the hint to leave me alone, and realizes that I am actually getting a little upset at this point.

Now, the husband disappears into another room and the Mrs. steps back about four feet. It takes me just a couple of minutes to find that the timer is bad and I will have to order one. I give her an estimate and a copy of the invoice and tell her I can make my way out to the front door, and I will call her when the part comes in. On the way out I am just amazed and baffled about the situation I was just involved in, a husband who likes to watch his wife tease or I don't know what! I figured they must be swingers and wanted me to join in, which I was not prepared to do at this time.

Housewives & Repairmen
"the Untold Secrets"
True Stories as they actually happened!
Husbands leave for work and their wives stay home to be "Serviced"!!

Big-Uns

I had been doing service as a technician for a couple of years now, when I was to be amused and embarrassed all at the same time while doing what seemed to be a routine service call on a washing machine that was making a screeching noise.

It was a very cold day in Livonia, Michigan as I started my service route for the day. All was going well, when I was on my way to my second to last service call of the day. I had just called the customer to let them know I was on the way and spoke to the gentleman of the house. He assured me they were looking forward to my arrival, and they would certainly be there when arrived. I had some idea what the problem was with the washing machine from the short conversation I had on the phone with the customer.

A very nice man in his mid 40's greeted when I arrived, and he directed me to the location of th washing machine. It seemed that he was the only person at home at the time, which was fine with me. I figured I would locate the problem quickly, as usual, and resolve it. When we got to where the washing machine was located, I asked the customer several questions about when the noise started, what size load it was,

28

Housewives & Repairmen
"the Untold Secrets"
True Stories as they actually happened!
Husbands leave for work and their wives stay home to be "Serviced"!!

and all the pertinent questions asked to give some idea how the problem may have occurred. He mentioned that his wife had been doing a very light load of her lingerie, and that it definitely couldn't be a problem caused by a small, light load, such as that. This explanation produced a slight grin upon my face, with which he prodded me for an explanation about why I was grinning and what I was thinking. I mentioned to him that I had a very good idea, even before running the washer and hearing the noise, what was most likely causing the noise, he was describing. He was kind of astonished, that I could be so confident from the few questions that I had asked him, that I might know what the problem was with the washer already. I told him to trust me and in a few minutes, after running the washer, I would let him know for sure what the problem was with the machine. He told me that he would leave me alone to work and he would be right back.

I walked in front of the washing machine, and reached up to the control panel to turn it on. The customer had mentioned that it only made the noise in the spin cycle, so I advanced the timer to the spin cycle and turned the washer on. Right away I heard the screeching noise he had described so eloquently, and reached up and

Housewives & Repairmen
the Untold Secrets
True Stories as they actually happened!
Husbands leave for work and their wives stay home to be "Serviced"!!

turned the washer off. I pulled out my pocket maglite and raised the lid to the washer. I turned the maglite on and leaned forward to look down inside the tub so I could see the holes that are factory lined in the tub. I was looking for any debris that may appear through any of the factory holes, and as I was about through making a complete 360-degree search of the tub, I noticed something shiny. I was thrilled that it was as I thought, and would allow me to get this service call done so quickly. I reached down inside the tub, grabbed a hold of the shiny object protruding through one of the factory holes, and pulled on it to remove it through the hole. It resisted as this certain object always does, but with persistence and a slight wriggling of the object it slid out completely. As it appeared intact out of the hole and now in my hand I chuckled, not knowing that over my shoulder watching me remove the object was the customer's wife. She had been standing behind me for a few minutes and watching me remove the cause of the screeching noise from her washer. She had not seen what I removed and asked why I was giggling, as I turned around with the object in my hand and stated that I had never seen one of these this big get stuck between the tubs before. When she noticed what I was holding in my

Housewives & Repairmen
"the Untold Secrets"
True Stories as they actually happened!
Husbands leave for work and their wives stay home to be "Serviced"!!

hand, she turned bright red with embarrassment. I told her that it was very common for an Under-wire to come loose from a bra and create this problem, but I had never seen one this big work itself between the tubs. Well, that was of no relief to her as she walked away with the bright red gleam of embarrassment on her face. At this time, I turned the washer back on the spin cycle and the screeching noise was gone. Now I was wondering where everyone had gone, as it was time to collect for the service call. As I wrote up the invoice, her husband walked back into the room and asked me if I had been right in my initial diagnosis. I told him I definitely was and showed him the huge underwire I had removed from the machine. He asked me what it was, and I told him an underwire from a woman's bra. He said it figures that's what it was, cause his wife never spends much money on her clothing, and to boot, his two daughters are almost as bad as their mother. He stated it definitely was his wife's underwire because his daughters were not that large. I told him I had shown it to his wife and she turned bright red. He said he saw her face when she came in to get him to tell him I found the problem. He said she was speechless and didn't answer him about what the problem with the washer was, so he came right in to find out,

Housewives & Repairmen
"the Untold Secrets"
True Stories as they actually happened!
Husbands leave for work and their wives stay home to be "Serviced"!!

and was not surprised at all after seeing her reaction. We laughed about it and I collected the service call fee for the repair.

As I was walking out to leave, I turned to him and mentioned that I bet his wife starts spending more money for her bras. He agreed with me and we said our goodbyes and thanked me for embarrassing his wife. Once again, he told me how his wife never spends much money on herself, but that he hoped now she would start. All in all, this service call made my day. It is not too often that you can have such a fun time on service call at the expense of the customer. If everyday was like this service call, all day long would be the most pleasurable job anyone could ever have, but it just never works out that way.

Housewives & Repairmen
"the Untold Secrets"
True Stories as they actually happened!
Husbands leave for work and their wives stay home to be "Serviced"!!

College Stuff

It was a very hot day in Tempe, Arizona, and I was working around the ASU Campus housing all day, when I was about to run into one the most shocking, exhilarating, nerve racking and uncomfortable situations that I had ever been in while doing service. I had only been doing service for about a year, and was about to be initiated into the reality of the situations that service men run into when they are on the road and entering customer's homes for the purpose of repairing their appliances.

I had called my next customer to let her know that I was on the way to fix her leaking washing machine. I asked her a couple of questions about the leak in the machine, with which she told me that it had just started to leak and that it didn't leak very much water at all on the floor. She also told me it was located in the kitchen closet, and that it was a stacked unit. From the complaint and knowing this type of machine pretty well by now, I had an idea what the problem might be and it was not going to be a very fun job to work on with the washer located in a closet.

I arrived in about 5 minutes after calling the customer, and was walking around this hi-rise apartment building complex trying to find her

33

Housewives & Repairmen
"the Untold Secrets"
True Stories as they actually happened!
Husbands leave for work and their wives stay home to be "Serviced"!!

apartment number. I located the building number
and realized that she was on the third floor, so I
started up the stairs to the third floor. As I
reached the landing for the third floor, I noticed
very large picture that was framed on one of two
apartment doors on the third floor. It was an
artist's picture was of a nude woman, and right
away I was kind of stunned to see this hanging
on the outside of an apartment door. The door
that the nude framed picture on it, was the
apartment number where I headed to work on
the washer. All kinds of thoughts started going
through my mind, as I knocked on the door
hesitantly. After about 30 seconds, which
seemed like forever, the door opened very
slightly and a young girl peered around from
behind the door and greeted me. I thought it was
odd that she was peering around the door and
then I noticed one of her bare shoulders from
behind the edge of the door. I told her that I was
there to repair her leaking washer, and that I was
sorry if I caught her at a bad time. She told me
that it was perfect timing and that I should come
right in, and help myself to the washer, which
was located in the kitchen closet, just to the right
of the entrance. After she stated the directions to
the washer, she opened the door wider and
walked away from me to one of the bedrooms,

Housewives & Repairmen
"the Untold Secrets"
True Stories as they actually happened!
Husbands leave for work and their wives stay home to be "Serviced"!!

naked as a jaybird. I was blown away at the boldness of this young girl, probably only about 19-20 yrs old and undoubtedly in classes at ASU.

I waited until she reached the back bedroom and disappeared within it, until I proceeded in to her apartment, and into the kitchen where the washer was located. I am thinking in my mind at this time, I don't believe this!! I had to very quickly remind myself why I was there, and proceeded to open the closet containing the washer. I filled the washer with water, and was waiting for it to start agitating, when the phone rang. I thought nothing of the phone ringing, until I saw the young girl re-emerge from the bedroom with a bra and panties on to answer the phone on the wall by the kitchen. I looked in her direction as she walked toward the kitchen and she told me immediately that she was sorry, she forgot I was there. Now I am totally confused about what game this girl is playing, or is she that forgetful?

I turned my attention back to the washer, as she answered the phone, and turned it on to run it. I noticed right away that there was a small leak coming from the bottom of the washer. I thought for sure, the problem was as I had first suspected it would be, by the symptoms she had

Housewives & Repairmen
the Untold Secrets
True Stories as they actually happened!
Husbands leave for work and their wives stay home to be "Serviced"!!

given me on the phone earlier. I started to remove the front access panel, as she finished with her phone call. I watched as she walked back into the bedroom in nothing but her bra and panties, just shaking my head in disbelief. I removed the front panel and immediately saw that the pump was dripping water and definitely needed to be replaced to solve the problem. I needed to run out to my service vehicle to get the replacement pump. On the way out of the apartment, I bellowed out loud enough so she could hear me from her bedroom, that I needed to go out to my truck, and that I would be right back. She yelled out for me to just walk in when came back, which did not surprise me at all.

I located the pump in my truck and went back up to her apartment and let myself back in. I started to remove the old leaking pump, which usually ends up leaking a little more water out on to the floor, due to one of the hoses being very short. Normally this is never a problem, until today, as nervous as this young girl had already made me with her blatant nudity. Well, the worst case possible happened to me as the hose popped of of the pump after I removed the clamp, and the whole kitchen floor was flooded with the entire tub of water in a matter of seconds. I tried like crazy to stop it, but my hands were shaking so

Housewives & Repairmen
"the Untold Secrets"
True Stories as they actually happened!
Husbands leave for work and their wives stay home to be "Serviced"!!

badly, I finally succumbed to just cleaning up the water. At the same moment that I had just flooded the kitchen floor with the entire tub of water, the young girl walked out of her bedroom. I apologized over and over for the mess I had just made and tried to explain how it happened. She was not upset at all, and just told me she would help clean up the water. She was now dressed in a tiny t shirt and cut-off jeans shorts, which by first impression put me at ease, but I was only to be shocked more in just a very few minutes.

I had brought a towel in with me to clean up the normal amount of water that leaks when replacing the pump, but this was not even close to being enough help for the mess of water I had flooded the floor with. I asked her if she had some more towels to aid in soaking up the water, and she told me she would gather some up and return in a minute. When she returned, I was calming down about the way this service call had started, because now she appeared to be fully dressed. She returned with an armful of large bath towels, and handed several of them to me. We both started to clean up the water, and everything was going smoothly in the cleanup, until she stepped in front of me and bent over to soak up water on the floor. As she bent over I

Housewives & Repairmen
"the Untold Secrets"
True Stories as they actually happened!
Husbands leave for work and their wives stay home to be "Serviced"!!

noticed that the crotch of her jeans shorts were ripped wide open and she was not wearing any panties. I mentioned to her that she had a large rip in the crotch of her shorts, with which she thanked me for letting her know, and immediately bent right back over to continue soaking up the water on the floor. I repositioned myself out from behind her realizing she was doing this on purpose, which now made me very nervous again.

We soaked up all the water that had flooded the floor, and then she returned to her bedroom. She stayed in her bedroom the whole time I finished fixing the washer and putting it back together.

This was fine with me, because all I wanted to do at this point was to get out of this uncomfortable situation. This young girl presenting herself in every way possible to me sexually had made me extremely nervous. I was not there to do her despite what she may have thought, I was there to repair her washer and go on my way. This was probably one of the most forward young women in all of my years of doing repair service, which had made me very uncomfortable. She made it very hard to do my job in a professional manner, and my first thoughts after I left her apartment, were about

Housewives & Repairmen
"the Untold Secrets"
True Stories as they actually happened!
Husbands leave for work and their wives stay home to be "Serviced"!!

the danger she was putting herself in if I had not been a gentleman. In my following years of service, I was to find out that to many women present themselves in this manner when you arrive for a service call. I must say that I am glad that I was always a gentleman, despite her inappropriate actions.

Housewives & Repairmen
"the Untold Secrets"
True Stories as they actually happened!
Husbands leave for work and their wives stay home to be "Serviced"!!

French - Not Just a Bikini

It was another typical summer day in Scottsdale Arizona, when I started out on my service route I was in a great mood having done service for several years now and looking forward to the great customers that you meet during a regular day of service calls, as well as all the beautiful women out by the pools in the Arizona summer heat. I was about to have a complete eyeful from one of my customers on this fine summer day.

I was half way through my service calls, and everything was going very smoothly. My next call was located in an upscale neighborhood in North Scottsdale. I called the customer to make her aware that I was on the way to repair her dishwasher. She gave me some symptoms of the problem she was having with it, and gave me directions to her house, which I appreciated, because it was hard to find.

I arrived at her home about ten minutes later, and rang the doorbell. There was no answer after about a minute, so I rang the doorbell again. I waited after ringing the second time for about 2 minutes, thinking that she may be on the phone and she will answer the door shortly. Well, after about three minutes I started to get agitated, because I just called her and told her I was on the way, and now she is not home?

40

Housewives & Repairmen
"the Untold Secrets"
True Stories as they actually happened!
Husbands leave for work and their wives stay home to be "Serviced"!!

I noticed a walkway on the side of the house going back to the backyard. I walked over to the walkway and proceeded towards the backyard. I reached the block wall and the gate and called out over the wall for the customer by name. There was no response for about 10 seconds and I called out again for her. Right at that moment the gate opened and I was taken aback at the site of her in front of me. She was standing there with the pool in the background, with a white French bikini on. I was very stunned by her beauty, which made me forget totally about her not answering the door just a few moments earlier. She greeted me and stated that she would show me where the dishwasher was, and to just make myself at home while I was there. I told her thank you as we started our journey through the maze of her house to the kitchen where the dishwasher was located. As she stood in front of the dishwasher in that amazingly revealing bikini, she described the problem with the dishwasher again as she had on the phone. When she was done explaining the problem once again, I knew right away I had not heard a word she said to me, as she stood there in all of her beauty. I told her that I had a good idea what was wrong, and that I would let her know when I had verified the problem.

Housewives & Repairmen
"the Untold Secrets"
True Stories as they actually happened!
Husbands leave for work and their wives stay home to be "Serviced"!!

She left me alone to diagnose the problem with her dishwasher, as she walked back through the maze of the house to the backyard to continue her sunbathing. There was a window in the kitchen looking out on the back lawn as I quickly noticed. She had wasted no time in getting back to her lounge chair and basking in the sun, as I started working on the dishwasher. I started running the dishwasher, and found the problem very quickly. To fix it, I needed a part from my truck, so I walked back through the maze of the house, the way she had lead me in from the backyard.

As I walked into the backyard and onto the pool deck, I noticed she was lying on her belly and had removed her bikini top. Her absolute beauty was making my mind go in so many different directions with wild thoughts. Knowing I needed to get to the business at hand in repairing her dishwasher, I continued towards the gate.

She noticed me at the gate and rose up to ask me what I had found wrong with the dishwasher. As she rose up, she paid no attention to the fact that she had removed her bikini top earlier, and spoke to me without worrying at all about exposing her breasts. I explained what the problem was, trying not to appear as though I was uncomfortable about her sharing her

42

Housewives & Repairmen
"the Untold Secrets"
True Stories as they actually happened!
Husbands leave for work and their wives stay home to be "Serviced"!!

breasts with me, and proceeded to my truck. While out at my truck getting the part I needed to fix the dishwasher, I couldn't help thinking about what an amazing job I had. I found the part and went back through the backyard and to the kitchen to finish with my repair. Just as I was finishing the repair, she walked into the kitchen to check on me. She had since put her bikini top back on and I was ready to write out her bill. As I wrote out the bill, she started talking about her husband, which happens an awful lot to technicians. I was used to the subject of the husband being discussed by wives that we run into, so it was of no consequence for it to come up again. She was telling me about how her husband works all day long and how lonely she is during the daytime. I mentioned to her that I hear that story all too often from my female customers, and that it takes great commitment and sacrifice to achieve all that we have in our lives. At this point, I was not only getting a little nervous about her intentions, but also realized that I had several service calls ahead of me and would need to be respectfully short with this conversation about her husband. She told me she quit wearing her wedding ring during the daytime hours when he isn't home, because she really isn't sure she still wants to be with him.

Housewives & Repairmen
"the Untold Secrets"
True Stories as they actually happened!
Husbands leave for work and their wives stay home to be "Serviced"!!

Now, I am getting uncomfortable with the direction of the conversation, so I quickly finaliz the invoice. I told her that things can be difficul at times, but life is what we work hard for and make it, and to consider maybe getting away from the lonesome atmosphere of the house during the days and maybe consider getting a part time job to fill them. I explained that she would redirect her lonely feeling with new friendships, and that might be all she needs to solve her lonely feelings during the daytime hours. I also recommended to her that she should always wear her wedding ring during the day, so she doesn't give the wrong impression other men who may find her attractive.

I then collected the payment for the repair I had performed on her dishwasher, and she thanked me. She also made a point of thanking me for being such a gentleman to her, and for the advice I had given to her about filling her daytime hours and wearing her ring. I thanked her for her appreciation and the very nice compliment she had given me. I felt quite good for not only being recognized as a gentleman, but to have maybe given her some simple answers to not coming on to servicemen and resolving her marital problems reasonably.

Housewives & Repairmen
"the Untold Secrets"
True Stories as they actually happened!
Husbands leave for work and their wives stay home to be "Serviced"!!

How Else Can I Pay For That?

It was Duck Season in Detroit, and I was preparing for another day of service calls. The weather was very nice outside, warm and clear. It was a beautiful day in August and I was about to experience a new situation with one of my customers, which I had never experienced before. This situation will prove not only to be uncomfortable, but also create a gamut of emotions.

I was having a decent day of service calls when I reached my seventh call of the day that would forever change my opinion of married women. The service call was for a problem with a refrigerator, and I had just called the customer to let her know I would be there shortly. The conversation with her was quite strange, it was only 11:30am, and she seemed to be somewhat intoxicated already. As I drove into her driveway, she appeared at the front door behind the screen to greet me. I could see slightly through the screen door that she was clad in a bathing suit but actually; the real surprise was after I reached the door. She was not only wearing a bathing suit, it was a white French bikini, and she was not alone. Next to her was another very attractive female also wearing a white French bikini!

45

Housewives & Repairmen
"the Untold Secrets"
True Stories as they actually happened!
Husbands leave for work and their wives stay home to be "Serviced"!!

I greeted both of the ladies and told them I was there to work on the refrigerator. The owner, with slightly slurred speech, replied they had been expecting me and to come right in and tak care of them. Her response got my thoughts running wild with anticipation. What was I was walking into with both of these ladies wearing such revealing bikinis and drinking so early in th morning?

I accepted the invitation into her home, and followed her into the kitchen, as her female friend followed behind me. She explained that the refrigerator was not cooling properly in the refrigerator section, but that it was working fine in the freezer section. I listened to everything she said in describing the problem, and immediately had a good idea what the problem was, which I was very anxious to solve quickly. was difficult to curb her discussion directed at me, with her ever-growing sexual connotations. finally told her I better get started or I would be there all day. She quickly responded, that if I was there all day that would be fine with both of them, since their husbands were out of town duck hunting. My first thought was to get this service call completed as quickly as possible and be on my way to my next call.

I walked over to the refrigerator and opened the

Housewives & Repairmen
"the Untold Secrets"
True Stories as they actually happened!
Husbands leave for work and their wives stay home to be "Serviced"!!

freezer door to look for frost buildup, which would cause the problem she had described. As I was bending over to check out the evaporator coils for frost buildup, the female customer spoke up with a comment about how nice my butt was. Seated directly behind me at the kitchen countertop bar, both women could overlook me working on the refrigerator. I did not respond to the customer's comments, but I did hear every word that she said. After she made the comment about how nice my butt was, that was all it took to get both women going with more comments, each holding their newly poured drinks. Now, both women were making very suggestive comments about what they would like to do with my body, as I worked to solve the refrigerator dilemma. It now appeared the refrigerator had less of a dilemma than I did. I determined the problem to be the defrost timer, and turned around to let her know that I needed to go out to my truck to get the part, and what the cost of the repair would be. She told me that I didn't have to worry about the cost, that she would be thrilled if I would just take care of them the best I possibly could. I was immediately trying to figure out how I was going to be cordial if they continued to get more inebriated and sexually suggestive.

Housewives & Repairmen
the Untold Secrets
True Stories as they actually happened!
Husbands leave for work and their wives stay home to be "Serviced"!!

I went out to my truck and got the defrost timer
and a heat gun to melt the frost buildup. I walke
back into the kitchen where the two ladies were
still sitting at the countertop bar overlooking the
refrigerator, when the customer blurted out how
glad she was that I had come back to her. Now
am definitely wondering about how I am going t
get this service call finalized and get on to my
next call in a smooth manner.

I opened the freezer door to remove the back
evaporator panel to defrost the frost buildup.
They both started making comments that were
even more suggestive about what they would
like to do with me sexually, between the both of
them. I acted like I did not hear a word they saic
and continued to defrost the evaporator. I
finished with the defrosting, and replaced the
defrost timer and tested it. The entire time I was
finishing the repair, the two women were
continuously making comments about what they
are fantasizing about doing with me, while their
speech gets worse from their favorite alcoholic
beverages.

After finishing the repair on the refrigerator, I
turned towards the women and opened my
receipt book to make out the invoice for the
repair. As I was filling out the details of the repa
on the invoice, the sexual comments from the

Housewives & Repairmen
"the Untold Secrets"
True Stories as they actually happened!
Husbands leave for work and their wives stay home to be "Serviced"!!

two women continued. When I finished the invoice, I asked the owner what form of payment she was going to use to pay the bill . She responded that the two of them were going to make it the best payment I had ever received, with a lot of fun in her bedroom. I told her that we accepted Personal check, MasterCard or Visa. I thanked her for the very flattering offer, and told her that I really had to get the rest of my remaining calls done for the day, but maybe we could do it another time. I tried to explain that it was not a good day, as I had many customers that were waiting on my arrival to fix their appliances. She was quite taken aback that I would turn the two of them down, as nice and beautiful as they appeared to be in their French white bikinis.

She paid me by check and walked me to the front door. She appeared to be upset that I had rejected their advances for sex with the two of them in her bedroom. I told her to have a great day and to enjoy their vacation from their hubbies. She said she would, but it would be a lot more fun if I would stick around and have sex with the two of them. I told her thank you again, but I really needed to get going to my next customer as they were expecting me shortly. I opened the door myself, and stepped out of the

Housewives & Repairmen
"the Untold Secrets"
True Stories as they actually happened!
Husbands leave for work and their wives stay home to be "Serviced"!!

house, just wanting to get away from these two married and inebriated nymphomaniacs. I told her goodbye again as I walked towards my truc She yelled out thank you Sir in her slurred speech, just as I reached my truck. I kind of laughed at her calling me Sir now, and got into my truck to leave. After getting into my truck, I thought to myself what a relief it was to finally b out of her house. It just blew my mind that two married women could be so drunk, so early in the morning, and be so sexual towards someo they didn't even know. I felt I definitely did the right thing in turning the two women down, and am sure it helped with their own conscience, when they finally did sober up.

Housewives & Repairmen
"the Untold Secrets"
True Stories as they actually happened!
Husbands leave for work and their wives stay home to be "Serviced"!!

Hubby Hunting? Wives will play!

Once again, it was Duck Season in Detroit, and I was preparing for another day of service calls. I was just getting over the surprise of the two women that came onto me earlier this week. The weather again is very nice outside, warm and clear. I did not realize it, but I was about to experience a duplication of the situation I experienced with the drunken ladies coming on to me sexually just a week ago. This situation will prove again, not only to be uncomfortable, but also create a gamut of emotions.

I was having a very nice start of the day with my 1st service call completed, when I reached my 2nd call of the day that would reiterate my opinion of some married women. I was on my way to a service call for a problem with a clothes dryer, and had just called the customer to let her know I would be there shortly. My conversation on the phone with her was quite strange, since it was only 8:15am, and she seemed to be somewhat intoxicated already. This situation seemed to ring a bell from my previous experience only a week earlier.

As I drove into her driveway, it appeared there might not be anyone home. The house was dark and the drapes covering the windows were still closed. I walked up to the door with an air of

Housewives & Repairmen
"the Untold Secrets"
True Stories as they actually happened!
Husbands leave for work and their wives stay home to be "Serviced"!!

anticipation, from the sound of her voice on the phone, and the idea that it appeared I might have wasted my time if she had left before I got there. I rang the doorbell and waited for an answer for what seemed like about 2-3 minutes. I rang the bell again, at which time she finally opened the door. I apologized for ringing the bell twice, and she started giggling out of control standing in front of me, wearing only a very tiny sized g-string style bikini. I introduced myself to her and stated I was there to work on her clothes dryer. I mentioned to her that I had just called her to let her know I was on the way, as it was quite clear she might have forgotten that I called by the looks of her. It was only 10:30am, and she appeared to have been drinking already and feeling no pain whatsoever. She told me I must have spoken to her girlfriend that owns the home and the dryer, and giggled again. She invited me in, and told me to help myself getting them nice and hot again. I could tell she was inebriated, and was a little worried about her comment of making them nice and hot again.

I followed her into the kitchen where the owner was, who was also standing with a smile on her face and only wearing a similar bikini, only smaller than her girlfriends who met me at the door. I said Hi to the owner, and asked her what

Housewives & Repairmen
"the Untold Secrets"
True Stories as they actually happened!
Husbands leave for work and their wives stay home to be "Serviced"!!

seemed to be the problem with her clothes dryer. She didn't speak real clearly either through her giggling and slurred speech, but stated to me that her clothes dryer just didn't work. Laughing uncontrollably, she also told me that was why they were wearing only panties and bras. She said she hoped I could help them get rid of their panties and bras, so they could finally have clean clothes, and that we would definitely have a lot of fun doing it. I was not only a little bothered by this repeat situation in one week, but also laughing inside myself, and saying to myself...why me? I stayed calm and asked her to show me where her dryer was. I explained I would certainly solve their problem as quickly as I could, so they would have clean clothes as soon as possible. She told me there was no hurry, and pointed to my right where the laundry room appeared to be, the room right next to the kitchen. I thanked her and headed into the laundry room to diagnose the dryer, get it fixed and get out of there as quick as I could!
I noticed that the dryer was a gas dryer and that after turning it on the glow coil was not lighting the burner. The access panel to the glow coil is in the front of the dryer and I was bent over on my knees peering into the access panel to test the glow coil, when I felt a presence behind me.

Housewives & Repairmen
"the Untold Secrets"
True Stories as they actually happened!
Husbands leave for work and their wives stay home to be "Serviced"!!

As I turned to my right to see who was next to me, I noticed the girlfriend of the owner was standing next to me with her crotch at my eye level. I quickly turned my head so I was facing the dryer and asked, are there any questions you have? She asked what was wrong with the dryer, and I stated that the glow coil was not heating up to ignite the burner, and that it needed to be replaced. Her response to me was that she was heating up real hot, and that I could ignite her burner if I wanted to. I was now not only nervous, but also getting somewhat irritated by the sexual innuendos that were becoming apparent. I responded to her comment by stating, I had the part in my truck and would run out and get it so we could get the dryer working very shortly.

I walked back into the kitchen and told the owner that I had found the problem with the dryer, and gave her the price that it would cost to fix it. She stated that as long as I could get her nice and hot again, it didn't matter what it cost. I told her would work like new again, and preceded towards the front door to go out to my truck and get the part I needed. When I got out to my truck, I thought to myself how unbelievable it was that this could happen twice in one week. It was definitely exciting, but nerve racking at the

Housewives & Repairmen
"the Untold Secrets"
True Stories as they actually happened!
Husbands leave for work and their wives stay home to be "Serviced"!!

same time, because I was there to do a job, not the customer.

I returned to the dryer and resumed my position on my knees in front of the access door to replace the glow coil. Just as I got started replacing the defective part, the owner came into the laundry room and said that she hoped I was going to make sure she was really hot when I was done with her. I told her that the dryer would be just like new and her clothes would get dry very quickly, as usual. She stated that the hubbies were out of town hunting and that they were looking for some fun, with a cute and sexy guy like me. I told her thank you, that they were both beautiful ladies, but I had a lot of calls to do that day, but I did appreciate the offer. She left the laundry room and went back into the kitchen where I could overhear the two of them discussing what they wanted to do with me sexually. Now I was getting concerned, as it seemed they may have had too much to drink to take no for an answer. I finished the repair on the dryer and was testing the operation of it, while they were still in the kitchen talking about all kinds of sexual acts they wanted to do to me. After finishing up with the dryer, I walked into the kitchen and handed the owner the bill for the repair. She stated that the two of them were

Housewives & Repairmen
"the Untold Secrets"
True Stories as they actually happened!
Husbands leave for work and their wives stay home to be "Serviced"!!

extremely horny and wanted to please me to n
end, for being so quick, cute and sexy. I turned
towards the women and asked what form of
payment she was going to use to pay the bill.
Her response to me was that the two of them
were willing to pay more than what the bill cost
with a lot of sex. My response to her was that v
accepted Personal check, MasterCard or Visa,
and that I really had to get the rest of my
remaining calls done for the day, so I really did
have time. I thanked them both for the great off
of sex and for considering me. I also told the tw
of them I was very flattered and that maybe we
could do it another time, when I wasn't so busy
because today I had a tremendous amount of
work still to do.

She paid me by Visa and walked me to the fror
door, appearing to be dejected about their
sexual frustrations not being fulfilled. I told her
have a great day and to enjoy their vacation fro
their hubbies. She responded that they would
have a great day, but it could have been a lot
more fun if I would have had sex with them,
since they were also lesbian lovers. I told her
again to have a very nice day and turned to he
towards my truck. When I got to my truck, I cou
not believe in a million years that this would ev
happen to me again, much less, twice in one

56

Housewives & Repairmen
"the Untold Secrets"
True Stories as they actually happened!
Husbands leave for work and their wives stay home to be "Serviced"!!

week! Once again, I felt I definitely did the right thing in turning the two women down and I am sure it helped with their own conscience when they sobered up.

Housewives & Repairmen
"the Untold Secrets"
True Stories as they actually happened!
Husbands leave for work and their wives stay home to be "Serviced"!!

It's In The Bedroom

It was a very hot day in Tempe, Arizona, as I started another day of air conditioning service calls. Most of the air conditioners are either on the roof, in the attic, or on the ground. Occasionally, you will get a room air conditioner that is in the window, inside the house. It is hot the house, but not as hot as being on the roof o in the attic. This particular air conditioner was invoiced as a room air conditioner, which was welcomed.

I had called the customer about 15 minutes before arriving at her house, which was in a low income area. She answered the phone and it sounded as though I had awakened her from a sound sleep. I apologized if she had been sleeping, and she said that it was no problem, that her house was hot and she would rather ge her air conditioner fixed, than try to sleep in the heat. I told her I would be there in about 15 minutes, and she said she would be awaiting m arrival.

I arrived at her house, which was actually a small shack like building. I walked up and knocked on the wooden door, which I was afraid would fall off its hinges if I knocked too hard. After about 2-3 minutes, there was no answer, so I figured she had fallen back to sleep. I held

58

Housewives & Repairmen
"the Untold Secrets"
True Stories as they actually happened!
Husbands leave for work and their wives stay home to be "Serviced"!!

the door handle, as I knocked harder on the
door, at which time I heard some noise coming
from within the residence. I then heard a female
voice yell out to me to come on in, that the air
conditioner was straight through the front door in
the bedroom. I hesitated to open the door, as I
always did when a customer yells out for you to
come on in. I opened the door slowly, and
looked into the room as I was opening the door
wider. The place was a mess, and I did not see
anybody until I got the door all the way open and
saw the bedroom straight through. Once I got
the door all the way open, she yelled out to me
again to come on in to the bedroom where the
air conditioner was located.

I walked into the home and proceeded towards
the bedroom, which was right straight in front of
me. The door to the bedroom was open just
enough for the customer to see me as I walked
towards it. I slowly opened the bedroom door not
knowing what to expect, as I greeted her with a
hello. I was shocked when I opened the door all
the way, and noticed that she was still in bed
with the bed sheet not completely covering her
body. She did not seem to care as she greeted
me, and stated that the room air conditioner was
above the headboard of her bed. The only
problem I could see, was that she was lying

Housewives & Repairmen
"the Untold Secrets"
True Stories as they actually happened!
Husbands leave for work and their wives stay home to be "Serviced"!!

there in the bed with nothing covering her bare breasts, and that the air conditioner was above the headboard of the bed. I told her that she would have to cover herself up, and I would have to move the bed so I could get to the air conditioner to work on it. She told me that would not be a problem, and promptly removed her sheet and got out of her bed, which made it obvious now that she was not wearing anything at all. She did not seem to be bothered at all by just parading around naked, so I did not let it appear that it affected me either. She walked over to her dresser, and started to get dressed, which made me feel much better. I moved the bed and started to diagnose her air conditioner, which was a very quick diagnosis. I told her that the compressor was bad and that it would cost more to repair the air conditioner than to replace it.

I moved the bed back to its original position, and walked into the front room that leads outside to write up the invoice for the service call. She walked into the front room where I was writing up the invoice, with not much more on than when I arrived. I collected the service call, and gave her some advice on places to go to get a replacement air conditioner, new and used, while she stood there with the biggest and hardest

Housewives & Repairmen
"the Untold Secrets"
True Stories as they actually happened!
Husbands leave for work and their wives stay home to be "Serviced"!!

nipples showing through her tube top, that I had ever seen. At this point, I was in quite a hurry to get out of her house as soon as possible. I told her to have a great day and I walked out the front door towards my truck.

As I was walking out to the truck, I was talking to myself, not believing how bold some women can be with their lack of modesty. I also thought about the fact that this woman had no idea who would be walking into her home, and I was glad that it was I and not some rapist, or worse, for her sake. I was quite shocked by the whole situation she had put herself in, not knowing who might be walking through her door.

Housewives & Repairmen
"the Untold Secrets"
True Stories as they actually happened!
Husbands leave for work and their wives stay home to be "Serviced"!!

You Want A Drink?

It was a very cool winter day in Scottsdale, Arizona, as I started another day of service call. I had several calls to make and was in a very good mood and looking forward to my day. My calls consisted of just about every type of appliance; dishwashers, washers, microwaves, refrigerators & heaters. I got an early start, and headed out for my first service call after stopping to get coffee at the closest convenience store. I called my first customer about 15 minutes before arriving at her house. She answered the phone and it sounded as though I may have awakened her. I apologized if she had been sleeping, and she stated she had been up for several hours reading the paper. I told her I would be there in just a few minutes, and she said she would be awaiting my arrival.

I arrived at her house, which was a beautiful ranch style house in North Scottsdale, with a circle drive. I pulled into the drive and parked in front of the front door. I walked up to the door and rang the doorbell, which sounded something like a symphony playing in the background. The bell finally quit playing and the huge entry door started to slowly open. The very beautiful woman standing in front of me in a white satin robe pleasantly surprised me. I greeted her and

Housewives & Repairmen
"the Untold Secrets"
True Stories as they actually happened!
Husbands leave for work and their wives stay home to be "Serviced"!!

introduced myself, as she invited me in and proceeded to show me where the kitchen was in this maze of a house.

When we reached the kitchen, she showed me which of the two dishwashers was leaking. I asked her to describe the details of what was occurring with the dishwasher. She stated that it was leaking from underneath the dishwasher and leaving quite a bit of water on the floor after the cycle was finished. I thanked her for sharing the details about the leaking dishwasher, and assured her that I would assess the problem and determine in a few minutes what was causing the leak. As I turned away from he r to start diagnosing the leaking dishwasher, she told me that was fine and that she was going to continue reading her newspaper. After several minutes, the dishwasher was still not leaking, so I knew at this point I would need to run a complete cycle to identify the leak. This also led me to believe from experience, and the brand of dishwasher, what the possible causes of the leaking might be. I was now laying on the floor in front of the dishwasher, peering under the front access panel with a flashlight, waiting for the dishwasher to present the leak to me.

As I was waiting for the dishwasher to start leaking, I noticed that the customer who had

Housewives & Repairmen
"the Untold Secrets"
True Stories as they actually happened!
Husbands leave for work and their wives stay home to be "Serviced"!!

been reading the newspaper, was now folding i
up. It appeared she was finished reading, and I
still could not help but notice how beautiful she
was. She noticed me looking at her, so I smiled
and asked her about the news for the day she
had just read. She stated that it was always bac
news and that she doesn't know why she
continues to read it everyday.

She started talking about how her husband is th
one that gets the paper and never reads it. She
mentioned that her husband had been gone for
weeks in Europe doing business, and how muc
she hates being alone. I agreed with her that it
must be rough being alone, and that I wouldn't
like it either. She then asked me if I wanted a
drink of water, and I accepted not knowing wha
was going to happen next. I was still lying on m
back on the floor at the base of the dishwasher,
as she walked towards me and straddled my
chest with her legs as she reached up into the
cabinet to get a glass. I just about died as I
peeked up inside her robe, as she stood over tc
of me, realizing she had nothing on under her
satin robe. I felt an immediate tightening in my
pants, as I started to show the excitement that
she no doubt knew she would give me by
stepping over top of me. Once again, she caugl
me looking up inside her robe, smiled at me anc

Housewives & Repairmen
"the Untold Secrets"
True Stories as they actually happened!
Husbands leave for work and their wives stay home to be "Serviced"!!

then looked down to notice my excitement she had caused. I was embarrassed, and excited at the same time, trying to figure out what I was going to do about the situation.

She then walked over to the refrigerator and got a bottle of water out of the refrigerator, and filled the glass. She walked back over to me, handed me the glass of water with a very big smile on her face, and said that she hoped I enjoyed it. I told her nervously, that I liked this kind of bottled water very much, knowing very well what she really meant. All I could think about from that point forward was that I had to walk myself gingerly out of this predicament. I did not believe in being involved with a married woman, but it sure did not seem to be of concern to her that she was married. After a little small talk, I directed myself back to the dishwasher as not to upset her.

I detected the leaking very shortly after guiding my attention back to the dishwasher, and told the customer that the dishwasher would need a new pump & motor assembly, which I carried on my truck. She told me if it needed a pump, then a pump it must be. I almost died again, as I realized this lady was not going to give up until she got what she wanted to take care of her sexual frustrations of her husband being gone

Housewives & Repairmen
"the Untold Secrets"
True Stories as they actually happened!
Husbands leave for work and their wives stay home to be "Serviced"!!

for 2 weeks. I told her I would be right back, as I ran out to my truck to get the part to fix the dishwasher.

As I was outside going through my truck to locate the pump & motor assembly, I knew I would have to use finesse to get myself out of this situation and not upset her. After locating the part, and preparing my plan to let her down very lightly, I headed back in the house towards the kitchen. As I reached the kitchen, I noticed that she was now standing at the sink with her back to me, so I readdressed my presence. She turned around and her robe was now gaping wide open, and she was not doing anything to close it. I told her I had the part and that I would get started with replacing it.

I started to remove the pump & motor from the dishwasher and she went and sat down at the table again, closing her robe slightly. I got the part replaced and tested the dishwasher, while I continued carrying on small talk with her. I tried very hard to direct the conversation away from sex and her husband. After some resisting on her part, she got the idea that I was not being rude to her, but I instead respected the fact that she was married. She also appeared to be getting the idea that I could not engage in anything sexual with her, with all due respect to

Housewives & Repairmen
"the Untold Secrets"
True Stories as they actually happened!
Husbands leave for work and their wives stay home to be "Serviced"!!

her marriage commitment to her husband.
She finally accepted my respect for her and her
marriage and left the subject alone. I could tell
she was a little frustrated by my declining her
advances, but also that she had great respect for
me and the way I felt on the subject of marriage
and commitment. I had shared with her that I had
cheated once when I was married, and that I had
promised myself, not only would I never do that
to another woman, but also would never carry on
with anyone else that was married. She gave me
a big smile and said that she understood, and
that she was sorry to have put me in that
situation. I told her it was quite flattering to me
that a woman as beautiful as she was, would be
attracted to me enough to think of being with me
sexually. I also told her that she could be
reassured that I would not say a word about it to
anyone, until now. It has been about ten years
since that day and all that matters is you know
who you are. You may or may not have shared
this with your husband by now but one thing is
for sure, he will not find out from me.

Housewives & Repairmen
"the Untold Secrets"
True Stories as they actually happened!
Husbands leave for work and their wives stay home to be "Serviced"!!

Not Behind Me!

It was a very warm summer day in Tempe,
Arizona, as I started another day of service cal
I had overslept, so I was not in a very good
mood to start the day. I had several calls this d
and was already behind schedule. My schedule
appeared to be full for the day, but they all
seemed to be straightforward calls by the
descriptions of the complaints.

I finished up with my first customer, which was
an installation problem that I corrected in just a
matter of minutes. I placed a call to my 2nd
customer, and let him know that I was on the
way. He sounded kind of feminine, but that did
bother me, as I usually get along with everyone
just the same. So, I headed towards his
residence, and arrived in about 10 minutes. Th
house was very well kept outside with flowers o
the sides of the yard and under the windowsills
pulled up in the driveway, got out of the truck,
and walked up to the front door. I rang the
doorbell, which was a mellow sounding chime
and the door opened in a flash.

I was kind of startled by the appearance of the
guy that answered the door, but kept it inside
myself not to let him be aware of it. He was
wearing a pink tank top that was cutoff above t
belly button, socks with sandals and very tight

Housewives & Repairmen
"the Untold Secrets"
True Stories as they actually happened!
Husbands leave for work and their wives stay home to be "Serviced"!!

cutoff short shorts. I told him I was there to work on his clothes washer, and he invited me in to take a look at the washer.

I told him I would be just a few minutes and that I would let him know when I needed to talk to him about what was wrong. I normally will tell a customer this if I want them to leave me alone while I am working. They usually get the hint, go into the other room, and continue doing whatever they were doing before I arrived, but this did not work with this gentleman. He stayed right behind me the whole time I was diagnosing the washing machine, not saying a word, which made me very uncomfortable for a few reasons. Number one; he appeared to be gay and was standing behind me, which made me nervous. Number two; he just stood there not saying a word. I was wondering what he was doing while standing right behind me, and I wasn't about to look. I always get along just fine with gay men, even though I am a heterosexual man, but this guy was giving me a very creepy feeling.

I hadn't noticed earlier, until I finished diagnosing the washing machine, but right above the washing machine was a calendar with pictures of naked men. Now I was definitely uncomfortable, and I was thinking to myself that maybe he was waiting for me to notice the calendar and say

Housewives & Repairmen
"the Untold Secrets"
True Stories as they actually happened!
Husbands leave for work and their wives stay home to be "Serviced"!!

something. Well, I wasn't even going to acknowledge it, and I didn't.

I turned around and told this gentleman that the washing machine needed a mixing valve, and that I had the part and could have it fixed in a matter of minutes. I also asked him if I could use his phone, as the office had just paged me. He then directed me to the phone in the kitchen, which was around the corner from the washing machine. When I saw the phone, I was now questioning whether this guy was gay or if he was a cross dresser. The phone was in the shape of a woman's high heel shoe. Needless t say, it took some control on my part to keep from laughing at the phone, but to each his own I always say. The phone was quite difficult to use holding the heel to my ear and talking into the opening of the shoe, where you would slide your foot into the shoe. I hurriedly finished my phone call and went outside to my truck to get the part to fix his washing machine.

I returned to the washer and finished the repair, with the naked guys in the calendar above the washer, leering over my shoulder. I could not wait to get out of this house. I had made sure th washing machine was working fine and the guy who had been very nice to me, paid me by cash I gave him a receipt and proceeded out to my truck, wishing him a great day.

Housewives & Repairmen
"the Untold Secrets"
True Stories as they actually happened!
Husbands leave for work and their wives stay home to be "Serviced"!!

Pregnant & Hormonal

It was a very hot summer day in Mesa, Arizona, as I started another day of typical service calls. It was mid July, and in just a few hours I was going to have one of the strangest days of my life. As I made it through all of my service calls for the day, I had only one remaining; I thought how smooth the day had gone. I was now headed for my last call of the day, and was worn out from the 118-degree heat.

I called my last customer to let her know that I was on my way to her home, and she sounded very excited to hear from me. I talked to her for only a couple minutes, which gave her enough time to share with me that the stackable dryer wouldn't dry the clothes, and that the vent was all plugged up. Right away, I was not feeling real good about the call, because some of the townhouse buildings are not vented properly for these stacked units, and it is almost impossible to clear out the vents. The only saving grace was that she sounded sweet, so I definitely would do my best to clear out the dryer vent for her. I told her I was on my way and that I would be at her place in about 20 minutes.

I arrived at her residence to tackle the venting issue, and found that it was a three-story building, with a ceramic tile roof. I knew that I

Housewives & Repairmen
"the Untold Secrets"
True Stories as they actually happened!
Husbands leave for work and their wives stay home to be "Serviced"!!

was going to have to get on top of that hot
ceramic tile roof to clear out the dryer vent. This
was not a very welcome site, because the
ceramic tile roofs get extremely hot when it is
118 degrees outside.
I knocked on her door on the third floor, which
actually curbed some of my apprehension,
because I knew that the vent was quite short,
being so close to the roof. When the door
opened I was surprised to see a short, very
attractive, young and very pregnant woman
standing before me. She smiled and greeted me
and I responded back with a greeting to her, and
introduced myself. She immediately mentioned
that she just loved guys in uniform, and that she
noticed me as soon as I got out of my truck. I
smiled at her, and just took her comment with a
grain of salt. She invited me in and showed me
where the stackable washer and dryer
combination was located in the hallway closet. I
assured her that I would find the problem and
resolve it for her, so she could get her laundry
done, which was piled in a huge heap next to the
closet. I started checking out the vent tube as
she went to sit down on the couch, across the
room, within eye site of the dryer.
It was necessary for me to get behind the dryer,
so I pulled it out a little ways, and we continued

Housewives & Repairmen
"the Untold Secrets"
True Stories as they actually happened!
Husbands leave for work and their wives stay home to be "Serviced"!!

to chat even as I was working behind the dryer. Her conversation kept leading back to her excitement over guys in uniforms, how sexy she thought they were, and how they really got her all hot and turned on. I was starting to get somewhat uncomfortable, knowing that she was married and pregnant, and still talking this way. I asked her what time her husband got home, hoping he would be home at anytime, since it was 20 minutes after six in the evening. She stated that she didn't expect him home for sometime, and when I was done with the dryer, she really looked forward to having sex with me. Man alive, I thought to myself, now I was extremely uncomfortable in her home alone. Not only was she pregnant and married, but also her husband could be home at anytime with her talking like this. I tried like crazy to change the subject many times, which she was quite aware of. She kept telling me how much I turned her on, and that she really wanted me to have sex with her. I told her that was not a good idea, seeing how her husband could come home at any moment.

Just as I was getting out from behind the dryer, after cleaning out the vent tubing, in walks her husband. I introduced myself to her husband, shaking his hand, and still feeling extremely

Housewives & Repairmen
"the Untold Secrets"
True Stories as they actually happened!
Husbands leave for work and their wives stay home to be "Serviced"!!

uneasy about her sexual comments right before he had walked through the door. He greeted me back, and then walked over to the couch and gave her a kiss, asking her how her day was. She told him that the most exciting part of her day was when I had shown up earlier. I almost died when she said that, not knowing how he was going to react to her admission of flirting. He joked that she is always teasing servicemen, and that I don't need to worry about her. He then asked me if I wanted a beer, which I took a moment to consider, and remembering that I was on my last service call, I accepted. I knew could use a beer after all of her sexual comments just before he had arrived home. The husband and I continued talking about several things, including the work I did, and his work in the medical field. Sipping on our ice-cold beers, we discussed how hot it was outside, and I also told him that I had fixed the venting problem with their dryer. He mentioned that his wife would love me forever, for fixing the dryer. He then invited me to stay and have dinner with them out on their patio, after we went for a swim in the community pool. Wow, was I surprised and very reluctant, but I felt safe knowing he was going to be there. We had a great time swimming and the dinner was excellent. We

Housewives & Repairmen
"the Untold Secrets"
True Stories as they actually happened!
Husbands leave for work and their wives stay home to be "Serviced"!!

finished with dinner on the patio, and went back inside their apartment to talk some more, where we were sitting on the couch. After quite a bit of conversation, the pregnant wife started having a very bad seizure, which startled me tremendously. With the husband's guidance, we helped her through the seizure, but the hard part was to come. When she started to come back to reality, she had no idea where she was or even who she was. He assured me that this was normal, and to just keep talking to her and reassuring her that everything would be ok. I have to admit I was quite scared, until he kept assuring me that everything would be just fine in a couple of minutes. She finally came back to herself, and it was like nothing had happened at all. He told me that this happens when she gets extremely excited, or stressed about something. I could only imagine that the actions of the evening had brought the seizure on, which made me feel kind of guilty. After things calmed down, I thanked them very much for the wonderful dinner, swimming and the whole evening.

I made my way to my truck, as it was now dark outside and quite late. I couldn't help thinking on my ride home, how this service call would remain in my memory forever. I was sure that it could never be surpassed by any I had ever

Housewives & Repairmen
"the Untold Secrets"
True Stories as they actually happened!
Husbands leave for work and their wives stay home to be "Serviced"!!

done, or would ever do in the future. Most of all,
was extremely glad she was all right, especially
after all the excitement and the seizure she had
just gone through. I learned valuable lessons
that evening, not only about life, but also about
how to take care of someone who was suffering
from a seizure. Whoever said a serviceman's job
stops at the appliance, was flat wrong.

Housewives & Repairmen
"the Untold Secrets"
True Stories as they actually happened!
Husbands leave for work and their wives stay home to be "Serviced"!!

See-Through!

It was a hot summer day in Tempe, Arizona, as I started another day of service calls. After working for so many years doing service, I had looked forward to summer days in certain parts of Tempe, especially around the campus of Arizona State University. It was always a good mood enhancer, to see all the college girls lying out on the campus and sorority hall lawns.

I got my route for the day and was pleased to see it was located near the University. This put me in a good mood right away, which I hoped would last through my final service call of the day. I had finished up several calls, things were going very smoothly and I was still in a great mood. I called my next customer's house, where I was going to work on a dishwasher. I told the customer that I was on my way to her home, and that I would arrive within 10 minutes. She said she would be home, and was looking forward to seeing me.

I arrived at her house and parked in the driveway, as I usually do when I am on a service call. I went to the screened patio entrance of the townhouse she lived in, and knocked on the metal screen door. I hadn't noticed, but she was right inside the screen door and saw me walk up and knock. The screen door material was

Housewives & Repairmen
"the Untold Secrets"
True Stories as they actually happened!
Husbands leave for work and their wives stay home to be "Serviced"!!

impossible to see through, due to the reflection
of the sun on it. When she opened the screen
door, I was extremely surprised at what she was
wearing. She was standing there in a long
nightgown that was completely see-through. I
didn't know what to say, as she stood right in
front of me, and didn't appear to be shy at all.
She greeted me, and invited me in while pointing
at the dishwasher, which was in the kitchen, just
inside the screen door.
I normally would have said something to the
customer about putting on some clothes, or a
robe before I came in, but the proximity to her
when she opened the screen door, was too
close for me to react. I accepted her invitation
and tried not to look straight at her, which felt
kind of rude on my part, so I tried to focus on her
eyes only when I talked to her. I told her I would
find the problem with the dishwasher, as I
quickly started to run it and kept the
conversation to a minimum. This was a big
mistake on my part, because as I started to fill it
with water, the floor began to flood. She told me
that was the reason she had called for service,
and asked if I was nervous about something
because I seemed somewhat jumpy. I told her I
had drunk too much coffee earlier that morning,
and that was the reason I was jumpy. I then

Housewives & Repairmen
the Untold Secrets
True Stories as they actually happened!
Husbands leave for work and their wives stay home to be "Serviced"!!

apologized for flooding the floor.

After walking into the other room, she returned with some large bath towels and handed them to me, as she stood there in that see-through nightgown. I could see every inch of her beautiful naked body through the sheer satin material as I took the towels from her. I though to myself, surely she noticed me looking. Well, she had, and she acknowledged my admiration by giving me a very sexy smile. I smiled back with great apprehension and nervousness, as my knees started shaking, uncontrollably. She said she didn't mind helping me clean up the water, as I took some towels from her, because she also had flooded the floor several times. Her assistance in cleaning up the water actually made me feel a little better, knowing that she was not upset at me for flooding her floor. As I proceeded to mop the water off the floor, she bent over directly in front of me to help. It was very apparent to me at this point, that she wanted me to see all of her through her satin, see-through nightgown. Now, with her completely bent over with her back facing me, I obliged her show, by admiring every inch and fold of her beautiful body. I was getting extremely hot and bothered at this point, and wasn't sure I could take anymore. I told her

Housewives & Repairmen
"the Untold Secrets"
True Stories as they actually happened!
Husbands leave for work and their wives stay home to be "Serviced"!!

thank you for helping, but I could get the rest o
the water, as it was almost all mopped up now.
She went over to the kitchen table and sat dow
after thanking me, and crossed her legs while
pulling her nightgown up into her lap. This left a
gap between her legs and nightgown that left
nothing to the imagination. I kept telling myself
had to get to work, or I would never get done
with this call, so I redirected my thoughts
immediately to the dishwasher.

I took the lower access panel off the dishwashe
and found that the tub had a hole in it, which w
not repairable. I told her she would need to
replace the dishwasher as I filled out the invoic
for the service call charge. While I was collectir
the payment from her, I could tell she was very
disappointed that I was going to leave so quick
I gave her a smile of recognition as I got anoth
eyeful of her great body through that satin, see
through nightgown. I also had mixed emotions
about how she had presented herself to me,
even though it was in her own home. I was
thinking to myself, that I couldn't believe that
women do this to us service technicians, and a
always, I looked at her left hand and sure
enough there was a huge diamond ring on it. I
didn't bother to ask her if she was married, as I
just wanted to get on my way. I told her to have

Housewives & Repairmen
"the Untold Secrets"
True Stories as they actually happened!
Husbands leave for work and their wives stay home to be "Serviced"!!

a nice day, and I left the way I came in, through the metal screen door out onto the patio.

Housewives & Repairmen
"the Untold Secrets"
True Stories as they actually happened!
Husbands leave for work and their wives stay home to be "Serviced"!!

I Need Something!

It was a very cold day in Buffalo Grove, Illinois, as I started another day of service calls. I have always gotten along with most of my customers except for 2 of them in 20 yrs. This day was going to prove to be a very different day for me in many regards.

I was to go out on my first call of the day, on a built-in refrigerator that had a simple problem with the trim on the door panel, as it was described on my work order. I called the customer and told her that I was on the way to look at her refrigerator, and to solve the problem with the damage to the trim. She seemed very upset, and told me she couldn't wait all day. I explained to her that it was only 7:30am in the morning, that she was my first call of the day, and that I would be at her home in about 10 minutes. I already knew I was not going to enjoy this service call, just from her attitude on the phone.

I arrived at her home, which is in Buffalo Grove, where there are a lot of residents that have more home than they can afford. From the conversation I had with her on the phone, I knew I most likely had one of these types of people as my first customer. I rang the doorbell at the front of the house, which she promptly answered,

Housewives & Repairmen
"the Untold Secrets"
True Stories as they actually happened!
Husbands leave for work and their wives stay home to be "Serviced"!!

stating I needed to go to the side door instead, and then slammed the door in my face. I started laughing as soon as the door slammed shut, knowing at that point that I was going to have fun with this call. I went around to the side door and knocked on it, she opened the door standing there in nothing but a very short nightshirt and panties. I am now laughing inside and rolling my eyes to myself, without her seeing me of course, because she is no sight for sore eyes. She told me to come in, pointing at the refrigerator, which was right there in front of me.

I asked her, as is practice, what parts for sure were damaged on the refrigerator. She snapped back at me quickly, that if I couldn't see the problem she wanted a new built-in refrigerator, and that she would get one because her husband is a home builder. I told her it didn't matter if her husband was a home builder, because our policy was not to repair damaged items that were caused during installation. I told her that home builders were aware of this policy, but I would cover it this time if she could please tell me all that was damaged on the refrigerator. She was not happy with my response, snootily pointing out the damages, and then promptly got her husband on the phone to talk to me. He stated the same thing about being a home

Housewives & Repairmen
"the Untold Secrets"
True Stories as they actually happened!
Husbands leave for work and their wives stay home to be "Serviced"!!

builder and had bought products from this corporation for many years. I reminded him of the responsibility of the installer towards damages during installation, but I would take care of the damage, regardless.

He hung up the phone with an attitude towards me, which his wife mirrored to a greater degree, as I continued checking out all the damage. I noted the damage on my invoice, and stated to her that I would have to order the parts, because they were not truck stock items. This is when she really blew up at me, stating that she had told the person over the phone what was wrong, and that I should have the parts with me. I told her that it was impossible to have all the parts for a refrigerator on my truck when there were so many different parts on a refrigerator. I then told her, as my patience was growing extremely short, that we would call her when the parts came in to set up a time to install them.

She jumped back on the phone and started dialing her husband again, apparently to have him yell at me again. I was not going to take anymore abuse from these home builders, so while her back was turned, I found my way out the door and to my truck, with her screaming at me the whole way. I got into my truck and started laughing at the way some people think

Housewives & Repairmen
"the Untold Secrets"
True Stories as they actually happened!
Husbands leave for work and their wives stay home to be "Serviced"!!

they can just walk all over a servicemen, especially when I was trying to do them a favor by covering the damage they caused during installation. Next to Engineers, that think they know it all, I would rank home builders, which will not take responsibility for damage they cause, in the same class. This home builder husband and wife found out that their intimidation would not work on me. I requested that someone else go back to her house when the parts came in, as I wanted nothing to do with a self-righteous, stuck up, Buffalo Grove, wife of a home builder.

Housewives & Repairmen
"the Untold Secrets"
True Stories as they actually happened!
Husbands leave for work and their wives stay home to be "Serviced"!!

Can I Help You

It was a very mild day in Livonia, Michigan, as
started another day of service calls. I was abou
to get a very refreshing view of a customer,
which does not present itself very often. It look∢
as though I would have a typical day full of
service calls. I had my morning coffee and
prepared to start my day.

I started my route as usual, calling my first
customer and heading to their house to repair
their appliance. As I proceeded through the da∙
everything was going as well as could be
expected, realizing there were always ups and
downs with customers. My next customer woul
prove to give me great faith that there truly are
great customers out there that make it a
pleasure to do service. I called the customer a∩
was on my way to work on her dryer that woulc
not start. In the work order, it stated that she h∂
tried to fix it herself and had taken it completel∖
apart. Even though this drives a service man
crazy when he has to go out on an appliance
that has been completely disassembled by the
customer, I was about to find out something
quite different regarding this customer.

I arrived at her home, walked up to her door wi∙
trepidation and rang her doorbell. She promptl∖
answered the door and greeted me with a smil∢

Housewives & Repairmen
"the Untold Secrets"
True Stories as they actually happened!
Husbands leave for work and their wives stay home to be "Serviced"!!

She had such a look of relief on her face that I was finally there. She was an average looking lady, standing there in front of me with a greasy flannel shirt on, which I had a feeling was dirty from her trying to work on the dryer. She was so funny from the second she let me in, apologizing for having to call us, saying that she was so sure that she could have fixed the dryer herself. By her attitude, I felt like she had some mechanical sense about her with regard to fixing things. My normal attitude towards customers that tear their appliances apart left me quickly with this thrifty lady. To keep things on a lighter note, I kind of teased her about tearing the machine apart, as I started my normal procedure of asking her about what her original complaint was with the dryer. As we reached the dryer that was definitely in a million pieces everywhere, she stated that when she tried to start the dryer, the motor would start smoking. She said she was sure the motor was bad, which is why she bought a new motor, but she couldn't figure out how to remove the old motor to replace it. I re-diagnosed the appliance to verify that the motor was bad, and I complimented her on her diagnosis. I told her that the motor definitely was tricky to replace if you had never done it before. I told her that I would show her how to replace the motor,

Housewives & Repairmen
"the Untold Secrets"
True Stories as they actually happened!
Husbands leave for work and their wives stay home to be "Serviced"!!

despite the fact that we normally did not install parts that a customer provided, because we could not warranty it. She smiled, thanked me for my compliment on her diagnosis, and remarked that she wasn't worried about the warranty.

I showed her the tricky part about the reverse thread on the blower wheel, which she was not aware of, and then showed her the best way to remove it from the motor. I helped her remove the old motor and install the new one that she had bought, and then together we put the whole dryer back together. We tested the dryer afterward, and everything was working fine. It was then, that a big smile emerged on her face. She was filled with complete satisfaction that she had just about fixed the dryer all by herself. She commented that she definitely could replace the motor all by herself the next time, if the need ever arose. This made me feel tremendously good, not only knowing that I had restored some of this ladies confidence, but also that I had shared with her some of my own personal knowledge.

I charged her the minimum amount I could for the time I was there, and told her it was a pleasure to meet such a thrifty and smart lady. She thanked me very much and we said

Housewives & Repairmen
"the Untold Secrets"
True Stories as they actually happened!
Husbands leave for work and their wives stay home to be "Serviced"!!

goodbye. I walked out to my truck feeling the best I had felt in such a long time, not only because I had given her a tremendous break on the price, but also to know that there are still such knowledgeable customers out there, even though you don't run into them everyday.

Housewives & Repairmen
"the Untold Secrets"
True Stories as they actually happened!
Husbands leave for work and their wives stay home to be "Serviced"!!

Shiawassee Place

It was a very cold day in Livonia, Michigan, as I started another day of service calls. I was asked to do a call on a room air conditioner in the middle of the winter that no one else would go out on. I did some inquiring about the reason no one wanted to go out on this call. I found out that it was a call that every technician had already been out on, including our great female Tech, and even she would not go back. The problem seemed to be that the guys that lived at this address apparently were very openly gay, and would come on sexually to all the male technicians. Each of the male technicians refused to go back after one trip to the home. Finally, our female technician was sent to look at the air conditioner. Apparently, they made some extremely rude comments to her, and now she was sure she would not go back to their home if I was the only one left that had not been to their home to work on their air conditioner, and I was told that I needed to solve the problem at whatever cost, so we didn't have to ever go back again. So now, it was my turn to meet these gentle men, with the winter air conditioner.

At first, I was somewhat confused as to why they would need an air conditioner in the house in the middle of the winter, but I was to find out soon

Housewives & Repairmen
"the Untold Secrets"
True Stories as they actually happened!
Husbands leave for work and their wives stay home to be "Serviced"!!

enough for myself. I called the home and told
them I was on my way to look at their air
conditioner, and that I would be there in about 10
minutes. The gentleman that answered the
phone seemed very happy that I would be there
soon. I was not bothered by the history of
service calls to their home, as it was normal for
me to get irate or problem customers quite often.
I took great satisfaction in solving situations that
no one else seemed to be able to solve. With
this fresh in my mind, I headed to their house.
I arrived at their house on Shiawassee Place,
and knocked on the door. Very quickly two
gentlemen answered the door and invited me in.
I asked them where the room air conditioner
was, and in chorus, they stated that it was in
their bedroom. I guess I should have expected it
beforehand that the air conditioner might be in
their bedroom. They both walked me to their
bedroom and showed me the air conditioner,
which was mounted in the window.
First, I told them that an air conditioner was not
designed to work when the room temperature
was less than 60 degrees, and that the bedroom
was now only 50 degrees. The taller one of the
two commented that it was usually much hotter
in that room, when they were both in bed. I
wasn't about to ask any questions regarding why

Housewives & Repairmen
"the Untold Secrets"
True Stories as they actually happened!
Husbands leave for work and their wives stay home to be "Serviced"!!

it got so hot in their bedroom, I just took his wo
for it. Secondly, I told them that the air
temperature outside also affects the operation
the air conditioner, and that the unit was not
designed to operate efficiently when it was zero
degrees outside. Thirdly, I told them that the
thermostat that turned the air conditioner on an
off would not cycle if it were too cold in the
bedroom, but that I could make a critical
adjustment to solve their problem. The last
statement about solving their problem, and
making it work was all they heard me say.
I walked over to the air conditioner, adjusted the
critical adjustment on the thermostat to always
stay on, and cycled the air conditioner on so th
would see that it was working. I wrote up an
invoice, collected the service call fee for the trip
charge, and told them that the air conditioner
would now keep them nice and cool.
They thanked me so sincerely, and walked me
the front door where I told them to have a great
day. Needless to say, we never heard from the
again about the air conditioner. I was not
interested in knowing why they needed the
bedroom so cold, as it was about 50 degrees in
the bedroom when I was there. It was just not
something I was interested in hearing about, ju
plain was none of my business.

Housewives & Repairmen
"the Untold Secrets"
True Stories as they actually happened!
Husbands leave for work and their wives stay home to be "Serviced"!!

My Husband Is Gone For Two Weeks

It was a very mild day on the Bluffs in Benton Harbor, Michigan, as I started another day of service calls. I was setup all day long with service calls along the Lake Michigan Bluffs. Each home on the bluffs averages in price from about a million to over 3 million dollars. These homes are extremely beautiful, but it always amazed me how they kept from falling into the lake, lurking right on the edge of the bluffs as they do so prominently.

I was having a great afternoon so far, and headed to my last call to work on a refrigerator icemaker. I called my last customer and a lady answered, who sounded somewhat older and very nice. I told her that I would be there in just a couple minutes to look at her icemaker and fix it for her. She was extremely appreciative and told me she would be home when I arrived.

I headed to her home, which wasn't far from my previous service call. I parked in the circle drive in front of her front door where I could actually see through her windows all the way to the lake. What a beautiful site of Lake Michigan it is for these people that live right on the Bluffs. I walked up to her front door, as I kept staring at the lake through the windows of her home. I rang her doorbell and she answered the door very

93

Housewives & Repairmen
"the Untold Secrets"
True Stories as they actually happened!
Husbands leave for work and their wives stay home to be "Serviced"!!

quickly, smiling and greeting me into her home.
introduced myself, and she invited me in.
She then walked me to the kitchen where the
icemaker was located.

I asked her to describe the problem she was
having with her icemaker, and she told me it wa
only producing hollow ice cubes. Right away, I
was aware of this specific failure, and told her
that I would verify what I believed to be the
problem and would give her an estimate to fix it
It was a very common problem with this type of
icemaker to have a bad inlet water valve that
would short fill the icemaker. I cycled the
icemaker manually and verified that the inlet
valve was indeed short filling.

After I was through diagnosing the problem and
working up an estimate for the repair, she
mentioned to me that her husband was in the A
Force. She told me that he was away for two
weeks at a time, and that she gets very lonely f
company when he is gone. I told her I could
definitely understand her lonely feeling, and the
it struck me that she was up in her years. As
soon as I thought this about her age, she must
have read my mind, because she told me she
was 67, and her husband was 62. I assumed he
husband must be a high-ranking officer in the A
Force, or something equivalent, to still be in at

Housewives & Repairmen
"the Untold Secrets"
True Stories as they actually happened!
Husbands leave for work and their wives stay home to be "Serviced"!!

62. I went along with her conversation about the military, because I had been in the Army for 8 years, so I could definitely relate.
I told her the cost of the repair, that I had the part on my truck and that I could fix her icemaker right now if she would like me to do so. She told me that it would be great to have her icemaker working again, since she uses the ice for her Scotch and waters. I told her that I would definitely fix it as quick as possible then, so she could have her ice cold drink when she wanted it. She smiled at my comment, and I assured her that I would be right back after going out to my truck to get the part. I returned very quickly with the part, and started to replace the inlet valve. As I was replacing the inlet valve, the conversation turned quickly to how badly she was feeling alone, since her husband was gone so much. She boldly announced to me how much she would really like for me to stop by sometime and keep her company. I didn't think anything about her announcement to me regarding keeping her company at first, because I was only 26 years old, until she told me exactly what she wanted.
The next thing I knew I was in complete shock. She told me that she loved the sexual company of a younger man, and that I was definitely

Housewives & Repairmen
"the Untold Secrets"
True Stories as they actually happened!
Husbands leave for work and their wives stay home to be "Serviced"!!

welcome to come over and keep her company anytime. Now I was extremely uncomfortable, a I hurried to finish replacing the valve and testing the icemaker for proper fill. As soon as I had tested the icemaker and verified it was working properly, I was trying to change the sexual subject she floored me with so bluntly. I tried to talk about the lake, the weather, anything but sex with this nice older lady, but to no avail. I started to fill out the invoice, as my hands were shaking noticeably and, which I hoped that she would not see. She was interested in having me as a sexual partner and she wasn't going to take no for an answer.

I finally finished filling out the invoice, and handed her the bill for the repair. She signed the invoice and made out a check for the repair, while never missing a beat about how much she wanted me to come by and have sex with her. She was now being very direct about what she wanted from me, knowing very well that I was finished with my repair and would be leaving her home shortly. I knew I would have to walk myself out of this situation very discreetly, without upsetting her or turning her down, by leaving some hope in her mind that I would come back. So as I continued to talk with her, I gently and slowly started to walk backwards towards the

Housewives & Repairmen
"the Untold Secrets"
True Stories as they actually happened!
Husbands leave for work and their wives stay home to be "Serviced"!!

door, telling her that I would definitely call her soon. I finally reached the door and opened it slowly, while she kept reiterating her lonesome desire to have me sexually. I figured I was out of the woods now, because I was outside of her door, and my truck was only feet away. She was relentless with her verbal quest for me sexually, even as I continued walking backwards until I reached my truck. Once I reached my truck, I told her that my next customer was waiting for me, and that I was running very late. She finally let up with her verbal attack on me, and made one last appeal for me to come by and keep her company very soon. I told her that I would, and that I really had to go for now.

After getting into my truck, I was just amazed at her determination that she was going to have me as her sexual partner, and that she was not taking no for an answer. It didn't matter to her at all that she was 67 and that I was only 26, she wanted me something terrible. The thing that struck me most as I was driving away, was trying to understand how she felt inside. It was hard for me to fathom the thought of being that lonely and that sexually charged, all at the same time. She was a very sweet lady, but I certainly was not interested in her sexually, especially since she was old enough to be my grandmother.

Housewives & Repairmen
"the Untold Secrets"
True Stories as they actually happened!
Husbands leave for work and their wives stay home to be "Serviced"!!

Come On In...

It was a very cold day in Detroit, Michigan, as I started another day of service calls. I had calls scheduled all day for the inner city of Detroit. I never much liked working the inner city projects because I was a Caucasian male, in a predominantly black project neighborhood. In the projects I was working, several service men I worked with had been robbed from in the past, so it always made me nervous when I had to go there to run calls. I always seemed to get respect from the young black children that would ask me how I learned to fix appliances, and I always took the time to share with them how they too could learn my trade. I know they really appreciated me spending the time to give them the information they were searching for. It also made me feel very good about myself, knowing that one bit of information I shared just might make all the difference in the world to a young child.

I called my first customer to let her know I was on my way to work on her washing machine. She seemed to be kind of short over the phone so I assumed she was busy and I told her I would arrive at her home within about 15 minutes. She said she might be in the basement so if she didn't answer right away to keep

Housewives & Repairmen
"the Untold Secrets"
True Stories as they actually happened!
Husbands leave for work and their wives stay home to be "Serviced"!!

knocking on the door even louder. I never liked this in the bitter cold of winter, because if they were in the basement, you could stand outside and freeze waiting for them to hear you knock. That was the reason I always called them ahead of time, so they could come up out of the basement and meet me. Apparently she was busy doing something that was too important to come up for 15 minutes and wait for me, so I proceeded to her home.

I arrived at her home, walked up to the front door and knocked loudly on both the metal screen door and the wood door inside the screen door. I must have waited for about 2 minutes, and then I knocked even harder on the wood door and on the glass window, as well. Finally, after about another 3 minutes, she came to the door and opened it. She didn't say a word, but just pointed inside at the landing to the stairs going down into the basement, so I proceeded in that direction. Just as I walked inside the front door and proceeded towards the stairs leading to the basement, two pit bulls stood up and started growling at me. They scared and startled me, as they apparently had been lying down on the stairs where I couldn't see them. I always carried a briefcase toolbox with me, which I now placed in front of my body to guard against them

Housewives & Repairmen
"the Untold Secrets"
True Stories as they actually happened!
Husbands leave for work and their wives stay home to be "Serviced"!!

attacking me and backed out of the house. I told her she would have to lock the dogs up in some other room before I would come back into the house. I could not believe she would walk me right by two pit bulls. I thought this to be complete ignorance on anyone's part to walk someone past two pit bulls that don't know ever know them.

I was quite agitated, and was just about ready to leave her home right then. She told me she would lock the dogs up in a back bedroom, which now left me standing out in the freezing cold again, waiting for her to let me back in the house. She finally returned to the door and let me back in, assuring me that they were in a back bedroom and that she was sorry they scared me. We then walked down into the basement as she told me all about the problem with her clothes washer. After we walked through piles of dog feces and urine, we finally reached the washing machine. The odor of the basement was sickening, which very nearly prompted me again to just leave her house, for health and safety concerns. I decided I would stick it out and deal with the awful smell, so I diagnosed the washing machine quickly and gave her the cost of repairing it. She told me to go ahead and repair the washer, so I proceeded once again out into

Housewives & Repairmen
"the Untold Secrets"
True Stories as they actually happened!
Husbands leave for work and their wives stay home to be "Serviced"!!

the cold to my truck to get the part. I let myself back into the house once I had retrieved the part from my truck, and went back down the basement stairs to the washing machine.

I replaced the part on the washer, tested it quickly and wrote up the bill for the repairs quicker than I ever had before. She paid me for the repair, and I couldn't get out of her house fast enough, knowing that the gagging smell wasn't all I had to worry about while in her home. I was hoping that those pit bulls wouldn't get out of the back bedroom, or someone accidentally let them out, before I left the house.

When I got to my truck, I really thought repeatedly about what had just happened. I just could not believe that someone would think it was ok not only to ask someone to come in when you have pit bulls running loose, but to have their basement be a bathroom for their dogs. From that point forward I always asked over the phone if they had dogs, and if they did, I asked them to please put them somewhere so I would not be bothered by them.

Housewives & Repairmen
"the Untold Secrets"
True Stories as they actually happened!
Husbands leave for work and their wives stay home to be "Serviced"!!

Over Their Heads

It was a very beautiful day in Chandler, Arizona, as I started another day of service calls. I had service calls scheduled all day in Chandler, Mesa and Tempe. There are always a very few customers that frustrate you by insisting that they know what is wrong with their appliance, bu they call you to fix it. My question has always been, if they know what is wrong with it for sure why don't they fix it themselves. I was in the Electrical Engineering program at ASU, so I have an idea where Engineers come from in their thinking. I was once again going to deal with the book knowledge of an Engineer this fin day, which I always found amusing.

I had finished about half of my service calls, so was time for lunch. The service order for my nex customer stated that I had to call them at work, 20 minutes before arriving, so they could meet me at their home. I contacted the customer at work, and he told me that he would meet me at his home in about 20 minutes. Before we got off the phone, he made a point of telling me that he had told the office what was wrong with the dryer, and that I better have the part that he tolc them it needed. He said that he found the push to start switch bad and that he told the office tha was what he needed to fix the dryer. I assured

Housewives & Repairmen
"the Untold Secrets"
True Stories as they actually happened!
Husbands leave for work and their wives stay home to be "Serviced"!!

him that I had the most common operational parts on my truck, and I was sure that I had what I needed to fix his dryer. He seemed irritated that I was not assuring him that I had the part he told the office he needed. I told him I would meet him in about 20 minutes, and I was sure that we would get his dryer fixed.

I finished my lunch, and headed towards his home, where I ended up waiting for an additional 20 minutes for him to finally arrive. When he arrived, he once again reiterated that he had told the office he needed a push to start switch for the dryer, and that if I didn't have what he needed to fix the dryer, he was not paying me for the service call. I assured him that we needed to go inside his home, where the dryer was, to verify what was wrong with the dryer. I wasn't about to tell him that the push to start switch just don't fail too often, so I didn't say anything to him regarding it.

We finally located the dryer, and I started to test the dryer to verify the problem, which upset him immediately. He asked me angrily why I doubted his diagnosis, when he had already told me what part was bad on the dryer. He then noticed that I did not have the push to start switch with me, which made him furious. I told him that I always verified the problem with an appliance, and that

Housewives & Repairmen
"the Untold Secrets"
True Stories as they actually happened!
Husbands leave for work and their wives stay home to be "Serviced"!!

it had nothing to do with doubting his diagnosis
then told him that the normal cause of a dryer
not starting was not a bad push to start switch,
but instead, it was most commonly a bad door
switch. At this time, I asked him what he did for
living, and he proudly bolted out that he was an
Engineer. I was getting tired of his badgering
me, so I responded to him that an Engineer do
not work on appliances, and apparently that wa
why he called me. Trying to contain my growing
agitation, and knowing very well why he had
called me out to his home, I asked him to pleas
let me do my job.

This kind of shut him up for a few seconds, unt
determined that the door switch, and not the
push to button switch, was the problem. He
immediately told me I was wrong, and that if I
didn't replace the push to start switch he wasn'
going to pay me. I stated to him that I would lik
to put the door switch in, and if this did not repa
the dryer, I would remove it and put the push to
start switch in as he had diagnosed.

I installed the door switch, which I had brought
with me in my pocket, plugged the dryer in,
pushed the start button and the dryer started.
The look on his face was worth a million dollars
knowing that he now realized he was not corre
in his diagnosis. He promptly tried to blame the

Housewives & Repairmen
"the Untold Secrets"
True Stories as they actually happened!
Husbands leave for work and their wives stay home to be "Serviced"!!

misdiagnosis on his meter, for inaccurate readings, and I just agreed with him.

I filled out the invoice for a door switch, which was quite a bit less expensive than the push to start switch, and handed him the bill. He didn't say another word about the misdiagnosis, or even the fact that the door switch was considerably cheaper than the push to start switch, not even a thank you. He signed the invoice and I collected the money for the repair. As he walked me to the front door, I told him to have a great day.

As I left the house, I couldn't help but saying under my breath, what a know it all some Engineers think they are. I didn't even mention to him that I too was an Engineer, as I find it just isn't worth mentioning with some people. I felt great satisfaction that I kept my cool, with such an arrogant person, which made my day.

Housewives & Repairmen
"the Untold Secrets"
True Stories as they actually happened!
Husbands leave for work and their wives stay home to be "Serviced"!!

Embarrassed Pink!

As I was going through my services calls, at the
beginning of another service day, I noticed that
had one for a dryer that would not run, but made
a hard humming sound when you tried to start it
From experience, this could be a number of
things from a bad motor to a child dropping
debris down into the lint screen housing. I
figured this would be a routine call as usual with
this type of complaint, and was looking forward
to it being an easy call. The call was scheduled
for the middle of the day, and I kind of looked
forward to an easy call around lunchtime.
So far, I was having a very nice start to my day
when I reached this dryer call, just before
lunchtime. I had called the customer and she
had stated that the dryer just wouldn't start, but
made a loud humming sound and then went
silent after many attempts of trying to start it. I
knew that this was one of just a couple things
from her description, and I told her I would be a
her home in just a few minutes to solve her
problem. She sounded like a very nice and
sweet lady, and I was always pleased to have
that kind of customer in my day. When I arrived
at her home, she let me in, and asked me to
follow her to the laundry room where the dryer
was located. As I followed her through her home

106

Housewives & Repairmen
"the Untold Secrets"
True Stories as they actually happened!
Husbands leave for work and their wives stay home to be "Serviced"!!

to the laundry room, I noticed that she had many religious items displayed all around her home on shelves and on the walls. I felt it refreshing to do something nice for such a nice lady of faith.
Once we reached the laundry room, she told me she would be back in a few minutes, and to let her know if I needed anything.
I started to diagnose the problem with the dryer, and determined there was definitely something that had fallen down in the blower housing that held the lint screen. This entailed taking the dryer apart to some small degree, but this was routine for me. As I was disassembling the dryer, the customer came back in to check on my progress, and I told her that something had fallen inside the blower housing and was stuck in the blower wheel. I told her that it was a very minor and common problem, because the opening to remove the lint screen is on top of the lid of the dryer and items periodically will fall down into the housing. She stated that she always leaves clothes on top of the dryer when she cleans the lint screen out, and that she hoped that it wasn't her fault. I assured her that it was common, and that a lot of times children will stick things down into the lint screen housing. She stated that there were no children that are ever around her place, and that it was probably

Housewives & Repairmen
"the Untold Secrets"
True Stories as they actually happened!
Husbands leave for work and their wives stay home to be "Serviced"!!

her fault. I was starting to feel kind of bad that she was blaming herself, and taking it so bad. I again reassured her it was probably just something small that had nothing to do with anything she had done. I also stated to her that sometimes it is a ball of lint that causes this same problem. She seemed to be a calmed by my suggestion of it possibly being a ball of lint, and left me to finish my disassembly of the drye After I had finally gotten the blower housing off, and located the object that was binding up the blower wheel, I felt kind of embarrassed that I was going to have to tell this very sweet lady what I had found in the blower wheel. I cleared the object out of the blower wheel, put the dryer back together, tested the dryer, and wrote up th invoice for the repair. The whole time I was reassembling the dryer, I was wondering how I was going to break the news to her about what had found in the blower wheel. I didn't want to make her feel even worse than she already did, thinking she had caused the problem. I figured there was no better way than to just tell her the truth, so I called out to her that I was done with the repair.

She walked back into the laundry room, and I was holding the object that had gotten caught ir the blower wheel. She got a bright red face, and

Housewives & Repairmen
"the Untold Secrets"
True Stories as they actually happened!
Husbands leave for work and their wives stay home to be "Serviced"!!

was extremely embarrassed, as she asked me calmly if the object I was holding was what was stuck in the dryer. I stated that indeed it was, and she started laughing as she told to me that she had been wondering where her pink panties went. She said she searched everywhere for them, and couldn't understand where they went. We both had a good laugh out of it, and my worries were solved that she was going to beat herself up over it. I had found a way to just make it a very light situation, and a funny one as well. She paid me and thanked me, and was still bright red in the face as I was leaving, which made it my best call of the day!

Housewives & Repairmen
"the Untold Secrets"
True Stories as they actually happened!
Husbands leave for work and their wives stay home to be "Serviced"!!

Customer Satisfaction
The Joy of Service:

There are many great experiences that a service technician enjoys while performing his job of repairing customer's appliances in their homes. Customers are very happy to see you when the air conditioner, microwave or other appliance breaks down. The most important factor to a customer needing assistance with a repair is, that the service technician be prompt, courteous and truthful.

Many customers have different histories of their interaction with service technicians, from great terrible. If a technician is prompt, courteous and truthful with the customer upfront, they are in a great position for a good service contact. The best feeling between a customer and a service technician is knowing that you have solved a problem for them and they are once again back to a normal working life.

Many times I have met customers that have had terrible experiences with previous technicians. was able to regain their confidence in the service industry by just resolving their problem in a prompt, courteous and truthful manner. The examples are too vast to list, but I would like to thank all the great customers that I ran into, in almost 20 years of service, for being the great people I will never forget.

110

Housewives & Repairmen
"the Untold Secrets"
True Stories as they actually happened!
Husbands leave for work and their wives stay home to be "Serviced"!!

To all the technicians currently working to help resolve customer's appliance repairs, and those of the future, I would say please be fair with the customer and they will be fair with you. Treat them as you would want to be treated yourself.

Housewives & Repairmen
"the Untold Secrets"
True Stories as they actually happened!
Husbands leave for work and their wives stay home to be "Serviced"!!

Customer Satisfaction
The Real Overly Nice Ones:

There are a growing number of customers that we consider overly nice. This can include the very nice lady that gives you a tip for just coming out to her home and not finding anything wrong with her appliance, to the customer that is too nice by coming on to you for special favors. The customers that are such a joy to work with are the ones that are extremely appreciative that you have taken the time to come out and solve their problem, no matter how simple or involved it may be. They are always such a pleasure to meet, so very kind and the type of people that give you a great feeling of accomplishment once you have solved their appliance problem, whatever it might be. These overly nice people are what make doing service a true pleasure. The other overly nice customers are not so comfortable to be around, and they have grown in numbers over the years. These customers are those that have some preconceived notion that you are their personal gigolo, and that by them paying you for your services think you owe them sexual favors. These customers always made me extremely nervous, because my principle was always such that I didn't mix business with pleasure. These oversexed customers can

112

Housewives & Repairmen
"the Untold Secrets"
True Stories as they actually happened!
Husbands leave for work and their wives stay home to be "Serviced"!!

sometimes be very difficult to deal with, without upsetting them. You must be very careful with these types of customers because they do not like to be turned down. Some of these customers will actually accuse you of acts that never occurred, or refuse to pay you for your service, if it appears to them that you are turning down their sexual advances. The best way to deal with these customers is to appear to go along with them, without admitting you will commit any sexual act with them until you can calmly and respectfully leave their home. Sometimes you have to make it clear to them that you must get all of your service calls done because other customers are still waiting for you to arrive. On occasion it becomes necessary, if the wife is just not getting the hint, that you leave them believing you will get back in touch with them as soon as you can. Of course, this just allows you to get out of their home safely with your payment for services rendered in hand.

The majority of these women from my personal experience are usually married women that are not happy with their relationships, which is a sad fact, but a very true one. These oversexed married women can sometimes be very frustrating and difficult to work with, which makes you wonder if they know the meaning of no. I

Housewives & Repairmen
"the Untold Secrets"
True Stories as they actually happened!
Husbands leave for work and their wives stay home to be "Serviced"!!

honestly did not enjoy going into homes with
these types of women parading around with
nothing, or next to nothing on and repeatedly
coming on to me sexually.

Another difficult customer can sometimes be a
single or married younger woman who is
extremely untrusting of a man being in their
home while they are home alone. A customer
that is a little leery of letting a service technician
into their home should be praised for their
cautious behavior, and not be misunderstood by
the service technician. Actually, once this type o
woman gains your trust, they can be a lot of fun
to have as a customer. The key is to always trea
the customer with respect, regardless of whethe
it is a male or female customer. These types of
customers are much more prudent about what
they wear and how they speak to you, in order
not to give you any wrong ideas about what the'
are saying. These cautious women are a
pleasure to work with, I must admit.

Housewives & Repairmen
"the Untold Secrets"
True Stories as they actually happened!
Husbands leave for work and their wives stay home to be "Serviced"!!

Customer Satisfaction
Not All Bad:

There are some customers you will run into that will not be kind to you no matter how prompt, courteous or truthful you are with them. A customer will react in a negative and disrespectful manner for a variety of reasons. I found out over my time of service that customers usually will react to a service technician in a negative way, because he is the first person they can finally vent their frustrations to. Usually, if a service technician gives the customer a chance to vent their frustrations, then reassures them that he will solve their problem, they normally will settle down, sometimes even apologizing for their disrespect. Don't always expect an apology from a disgruntled customer, as some will just not give you one.

I only had three customers over the whole time I did service, that I could not deal with reasonably, which resulted in my leaving their homes without saying goodbye. This is not unheard of, but always remember to try your best to make them understand that you are there to help them, and that you are not there to be verbally abused. One of my most successful responses to a customer that would greet me at the door yelling, was to state to them that I couldn't fix their

115

Housewives & Repairmen
"the Untold Secrets"
True Stories as they actually happened!
Husbands leave for work and their wives stay home to be "Serviced"!!

appliance if they didn't let me in. This normally works to quiet them down, so you can move on to the reason you showed up at their door.

One thing you need to remember when dealing with a customer is to never be rude, combative or threatening. You are there to provide them with a professional service and you never know what other problems they may be dealing with in their own life at the same time as their broken appliance.

Once again, always treat a customer the way you would want to be treated.

Housewives & Repairmen
"the Untold Secrets"
True Stories as they actually happened!
Husbands leave for work and their wives stay home to be "Serviced"!!

It's All Worth It
Personal Satisfaction:

The one thing that is most important in a service technician's day is the personal satisfaction he gains from providing top-notch service to a customer. There is great satisfaction in meeting most customers, diagnosing their appliance problems and most of all fixing their appliance. Many times you may run into a customer that has had many technicians out to their home before you have arrived, and haven't fixed the problem with their appliance. The customer is usually quite upset at this point and is leery of whether you will be able to fix the problem either. I really enjoyed helping the customers that have had several technicians out on unresolved appliance problems or were very irate for one reason or other. I would always reassure the customer that I was ultimately chosen to fix their appliance and by the time I left their home the problem would be resolved. My air of confidence to the customer would usually put them at ease, and if nothing else, it would at least convince them to let me in to prove myself. By the time I was done fixing their appliance, they were thrilled and would make me feel like the best thing since sliced bread. What a feeling!
The best feeling in doing your job, as a service

Housewives & Repairmen
"the Untold Secrets"
True Stories as they actually happened!
Husbands leave for work and their wives stay home to be "Serviced"!!

technician is the personal satisfaction you
receive when you see that big smile. That
feeling of relief on the customers face when you
have resolved the problem with their appliance i
one we can all relate to at some time.

Housewives & Repairmen
"the Untold Secrets"
True Stories as they actually happened!
Husbands leave for work and their wives stay home to be "Serviced"!!

It's All Worth It
Doing It Right:

There are many levels of experience amongst service technicians. One of the problems that can arise for some technicians is that they try to bandage up an appliance, instead of repair it properly with the right replacement parts. The reason for some of this improper repair seems to stem from the pressure of the customer to have the appliance working right now, instead of waiting for a technician to come back at a later date with the proper part. Another reason is the lack of proper training on the technicians' part to properly know how to repair the appliance. The third and worst excuse for a technician to not properly repair the appliance is that they are trying to cut corners and cost. The third example is not acceptable at all and lends to making a bad name for the all the good technicians in the field.

The only way to fix an appliance or any other customer product is to do it right the first time. Using the proper parts for the repair and having the proper training to diagnose the product is essential but unfortunately, not universal. This is specifically why; I very much enjoyed the position as National Trainer for technicians in order to give them the skills to do the job right

119

Housewives & Repairmen
"the Untold Secrets"
True Stories as they actually happened!
Husbands leave for work and their wives stay home to be "Serviced"!!

the first time.

Along these same lines, there is a very small fraction of individuals that call themselves technicians, but instead are just out there to rip off customers. This has been highlighted in new programs, such as 60 minutes, that have aired numerous documentary shows on these so-called technicians and their rip off schemes. Thi is an extremely unfair reflection on the majority of service companies, which are comprised of a very large number of honest technicians, and no the so-called technicians that these shows depict. The media creates a very unfair vision o the majority of the service industry by airing these programs. They also cause an extremely unfair bias of the entire service industry becaus of their programs, and their inaccurate portrayal of the average honest technician.

Housewives & Repairmen
"the Untold Secrets"
True Stories as they actually happened!
Husbands leave for work and their wives stay home to be "Serviced"!!

It's Been Such A Pleasure
Don't Worry Husbands & Wives:

For those husbands that are not aware of your wives indiscretions in the past, you are probably divorced by now, hopefully. If you are not divorced, either you have an open marriage or you are gone too much to know what your wife is doing behind your back. Though not all wives depict this type of behavior, it shames me from my experience in talking to these married women who wanted to cheat on their husbands with me while I was in their home to repair their appliances. The common theme always spoken from the wives was they were extremely lonely and unhappy with their husband for one reason or another. Wake up and see the sign husbands, unless you are too busy cheating yourselves while you are away. For those wives that come on to service technicians I would say to you all "Stop putting a service technician in that position". Deal with the problems of your marriage if you are not happy with your husbands, the solution is not to have an affair with a service technician. This not only puts the service technician in a very compromising position, but also allows you to bury yourself in the denial of your problem marriage for a just a few moments. You should go to counseling with

Housewives & Repairmen
"the Untold Secrets"
True Stories as they actually happened!
Husbands leave for work and their wives stay home to be "Serviced"!!

your husband and work through your problems
and differences, or get divorced.

Housewives & Repairmen
"the Untold Secrets"
True Stories as they actually happened!
Husbands leave for work and their wives stay home to be "Serviced"!!

It's Been Such A Pleasure
Thank You:

I would like to extend my thanks to all the great customers that I have had the privilege of interacting with and helping solve their appliance issues. I had a very interesting time, both pleasurable and difficult, throughout the entire time of my service career.

There are only about three customers I wouldn't want to see in a cafe, much less on the street, but the rest of my customers I would take great comfort in not only sitting at a table in a café with, but would take great pleasure in buying them lunch.

Once again, I would like to thank all the customers that made my service career such a pleasant experience!

With Sincere Thanks,
Michael C. Riley
Former Service Technician

www.ingramcontent.com/pod-product-compliance
Lightning Source LLC
Chambersburg PA
CBHW072201270326
41930CB00011B/2500